Crafty Dolls
Jane Bull

DK

This book is for...

... my husband, Stephen, and our three children...

Lottie, Billy, and Jim

Hello, I'm Jane Bull.

Hello, I'm Jane Bull.

Welcome to Crafty Dolls

Why not make a doll that looks just like you or like someone you know? How can you resist? This book is full of ideas to get you started. Have fun!

Design and Text Jane Bull
Photographer Andy Crawford
Senior Editor Carrie Love
US Editor Margaret Parrish
US Senior Editor Shannon Beatty
Designer Charlotte Johnson
Jacket Designer Ria Holland
Production Editor Andy Hilliard
Production Controller Ché Creasey
Managing Editor Penny Smith
Managing Art Editor Marianne Markham
Creative Director Jane Bull
Category Publisher Mary Ling

First American Edition, 2014
Published in the United States by DK Publishing
345 Hudson Street
New York, New York 10014
A Penguin Random House Company
14 15 16 17 18   10 9 8 7 6 5 4 3 2
003–192952–July/2014

Published in Great Britain by Dorling Kindersley Limited.

A catalog record for this book is available from
the Library of Congress.
ISBN: 978-1-4654-1957-6

DK books are available at special discounts when purchased
in bulk for sales promotions, premiums, fund-raising, or
educational use. For details, contact: DK Publishing Special
Markets, 345 Hudson Street, New York, New York 10014
or SpecialSales@dk.com.
Printed and bound in China.

A WORLD OF IDEAS:
SEE ALL THERE IS TO KNOW
www.dk.com

Meet the dolls

You'll need the sewing kit and other essentials for every project. See pages 112–113.

1

Lottie
Rag dolls

Lottie dolls

One pattern makes lots of dolls - Here's a simple rag-doll design that can be adapted to create all kinds of characters.

Doll templates and "how to"

The templates for making the dolls can be found on pages 14–15, including those for the body, hair, shoes, and some clothes. Additional templates for dolls such as Shelly the Mermaid and Cinders are included. Instructions for making the dolls are on pages 16–19.

How to begin your doll

1 Use the templates on pages 14–15.

For the body, fold a piece of tracing paper in half.

Place the paper over the shape and draw around the outline.

2 Keeping the paper folded, cut out the shape.

For other shapes, use a single layer of paper and simply follow the lines.

Open up the paper, ready to pin onto the fabric.

You will need

Cotton fabric
Any lightweight cotton fabric will work for your doll, as will muslin or linen.

Linen

Muslin

Needle and thread

FOR ONE DOLL you will need 2 pieces of fabric about 12in x 12in (30cm x 30cm).

Poly fill

You will also need...

• Sewing kit and other essentials (see pages 112–113)
• Tracing paper and pen to make paper templates

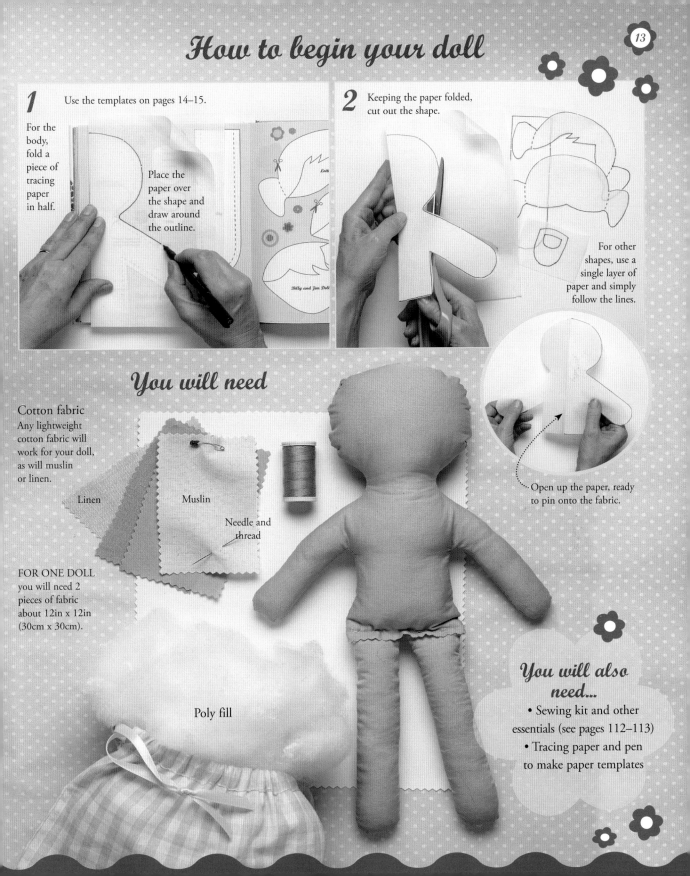

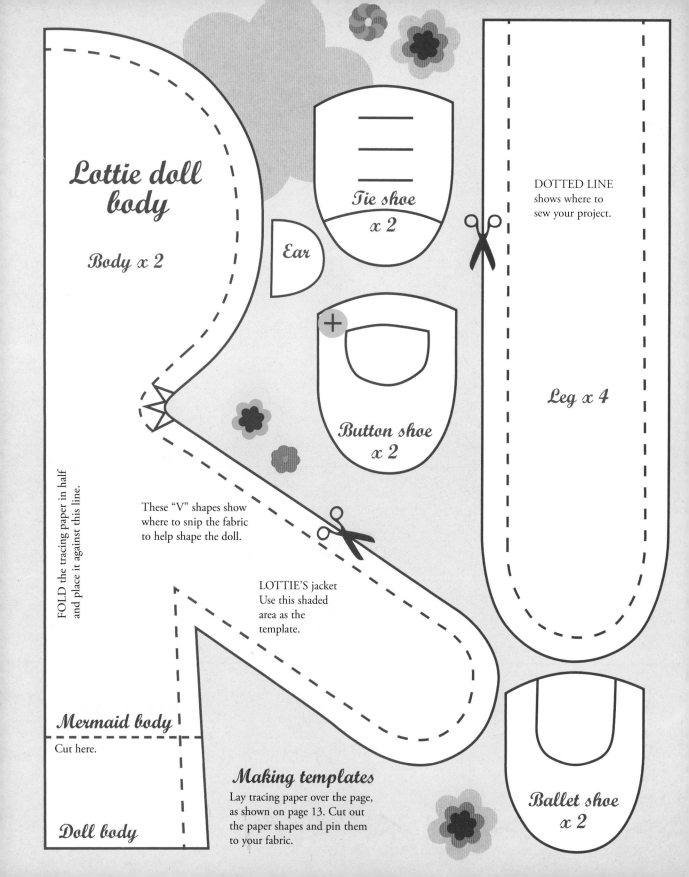

Lottie doll body

Body x 2

FOLD the tracing paper in half and place it against this line.

Mermaid body

Cut here.

Doll body

Tie shoe

x 2

Ear

Button shoe

x 2

These "V" shapes show where to snip the fabric to help shape the doll.

LOTTIE'S jacket Use this shaded area as the template.

DOTTED LINE shows where to sew your project.

Leg x 4

Ballet shoe

x 2

Making templates

Lay tracing paper over the page, as shown on page 13. Cut out the paper shapes and pin them to your fabric.

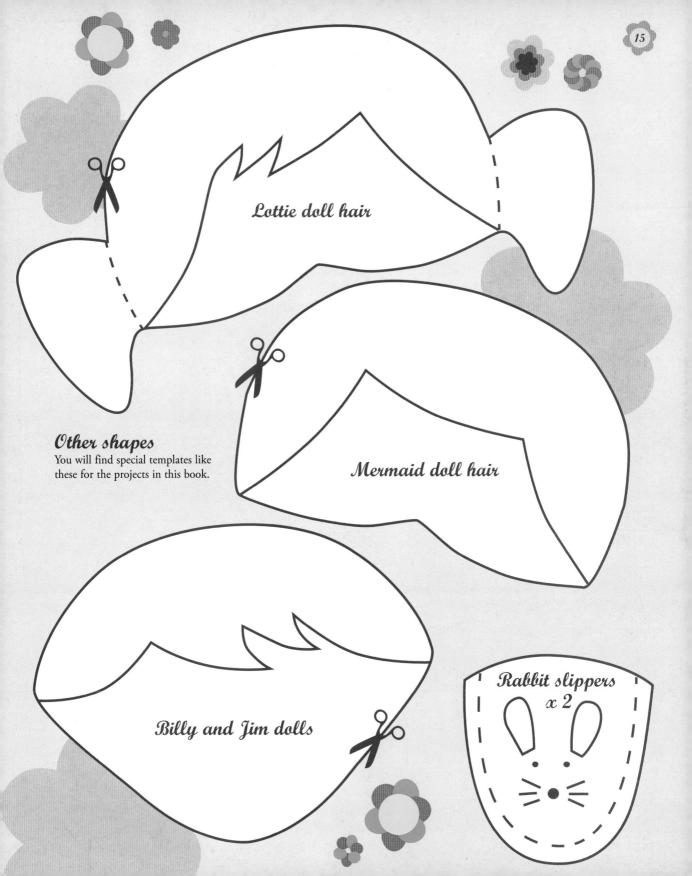

Lottie doll hair

Mermaid doll hair

Other shapes
You will find special templates like
these for the projects in this book.

Billy and Jim dolls

Rabbit slippers
x 2

How to make a Lottie doll

1

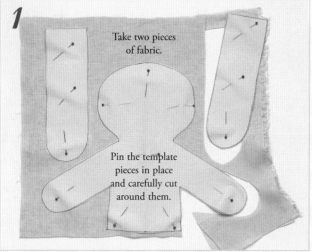

Take two pieces of fabric.

Pin the template pieces in place and carefully cut around them.

2

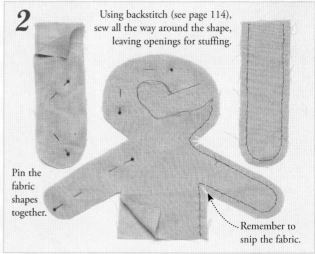

Using backstitch (see page 114), sew all the way around the shape, leaving openings for stuffing.

Pin the fabric shapes together.

Remember to snip the fabric.

3

Turn the shape the right way out. Push the arms through first, followed by the rest of the body.

Remember to cut the fabric as shown on the template.

Be careful not to snip the stitches!

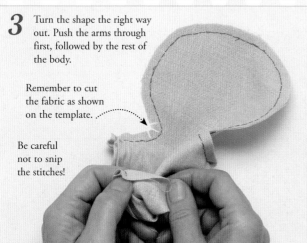

4

Turn the body all the way out, adjusting the shape as you go.

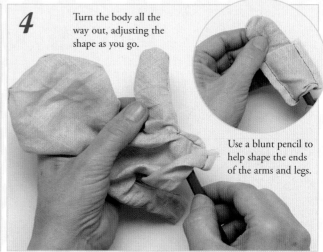

Use a blunt pencil to help shape the ends of the arms and legs.

5

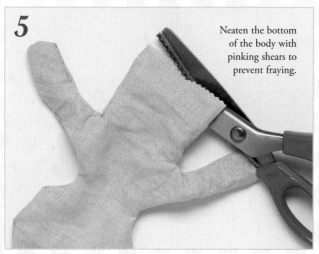

Neaten the bottom of the body with pinking shears to prevent fraying.

6

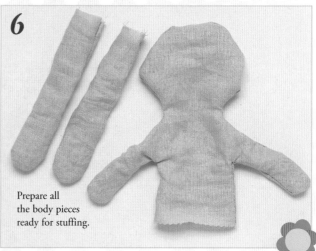

Prepare all the body pieces ready for stuffing.

7

Fill the body and legs, putting small clumps of stuffing in a little at a time.

Keep adding stuffing, working it into the shape with your fingers.

8

Work the stuffing into all the corners to make the body firm, but not overstuffed.

Use a blunt pencil to help shape the arms and legs.

9

All the parts are ready to assemble. Don't overfill them, since this will make it difficult to attach the legs.

I'm ready!

This is the basic Lottie doll. She's ready to be transformed as you choose.

10

Sew the ends of the legs together to make it easier to attach them to the body.

11

Pin the legs inside the bottom of the body and sew securely in place.

NOTE: The body for Shelly the Mermaid is cut shorter than the Lottie doll.

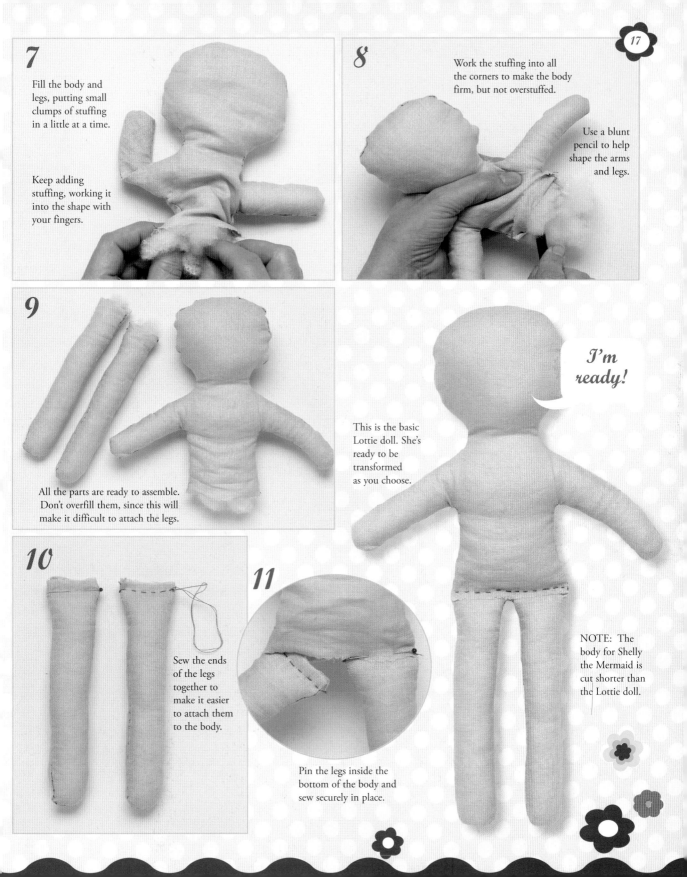

Making hair and faces

Each of your dolls can have a different color of hair styled any way you like. Here's how to make the hair and attach it to the doll's head. For the face, pencil in the features, then sew over the marks.

You will need

- Sewing kit (see pages 112–113)
  FOR HAIR • Felt fabric
  FOR FEATURES
  • Embroidery thread • Pencil

Trace and cut out the patterns for the hair and pin them to the felt.

Cut out the hair shapes.

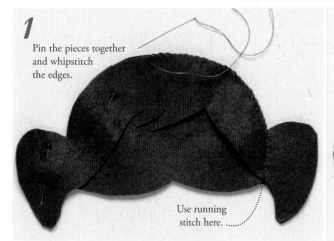

1

Pin the pieces together and whipstitch the edges.

Use running stitch here.

2

Continue sewing around the pigtails.

3

Fit the hair onto the head.

Adjust the hair until it fits snugly onto the head and is in the right position.

4

Sew the hair onto the head all the way around the back.

Draw a face

1
Lightly pencil on the eyes, nose, and mouth.

2
Knot the end of the thread and put the needle in through the side of the head.

Bring the needle out at the front and sew a few stitches to make the eye shape.

Bring the needle back out at the side of the head; cut off the thread and the knot.

3
For the mouth and nose, make small stitches and repeat the steps shown above.

Give her bows made from small pieces of felt (see page 20). Cut out the bows and sew them onto her pigtails.

Making faces

Creating the cute doll faces you want isn't always easy: Are the eyes too far apart? Is the smile right? Experiment! Lightly pencil in the eyes and mouth before you begin sewing.

Add ears
See the Billy and Jim dolls on page 24–29.

Cut out the ear shapes using the template on page 14.

Position the ear on the head seam and whipstitch it neatly into place.

Repeat these steps for the other ear.

Lottie doll

Lottie loves making crafts - With her scissors in hand and her knitting needles at the ready, she's all set to start crafting. She's a crafty doll herself - using this basic design, you can make all kinds of other characters.

What a doll!

Lottie is all dressed up for a fun summer day. Here she wears a matching blouse and skirt, a fitted felt jacket, and a cute little pair of felt shoes.

Find the template for the Lottie doll on pages 13–19.

Lottie's summer clothes

See the next page for how to make the clothes.

Red felt ribbons

Felt jacket

The jacket is made from three pieces of felt. The template is on page 14.

Blouse and shirt

These two items are in matching lightweight cotton. The skirt is gathered simply with a ribbon and tied at the waist.

Decorate the skirt with ribbons such as this rickrack.

Add tiny felt buttons using cross-stitch.

Felt shoes

You will need

A BASIC DOLL (see pages 13–19) • Sewing kit (see pages 112–113)
SKIRT and BLOUSE: • Cotton fabric 18in x 10in (45cm x 25cm)
• Ribbon 16in (40cm) • Rickrack for trimming
JACKET: • 2 felt pieces 9½in x 5in (23cm x 12cm)
SHOES: • Felt scraps for shoes • Buttons

How to make Lottie's clothes

Felt jacket

1 Make a paper template using the jacket shape on page 14.

Lay two pieces of felt on top of each other. Pin the template in place and cut around it.

2 Cut the front jacket in half to make a left and a right side.

BACK jacket

FRONT jacket

3 Using whipstitch (see page 114), sew the pieces together.

Blouse

1 Cut out three pieces of fabric as shown.

Fold over the top edges ¼in (5mm) and sew them down using running stitch.

FRONT blouse
4½in x 3in
(11cm x 8cm)

BACK blouse left
3in x 3in
(8cm x 8cm)

BACK blouse right
3in x 3in
(8cm x 8cm)

NOTE: Neaten the other edges with pinking shears.

2 Place the two back pieces on the front piece with the printed sides facing in. Whipstitch along the top edge from each end to form the shoulders of the blouse.

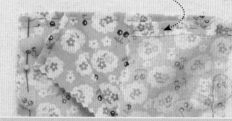

Sew up the sides with backstitch, leaving a gap for the armhole.

3 Fold over the edge of the armhole and sew the fold in place.

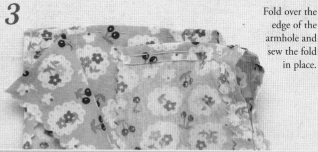

4 Turn the blouse right-side out.

Use a tiny safety pin to hold the back together.

Shoes x 2

Trace the shoe template on paper and pin it to the felt.

To add a button, cut out a small disk of felt.

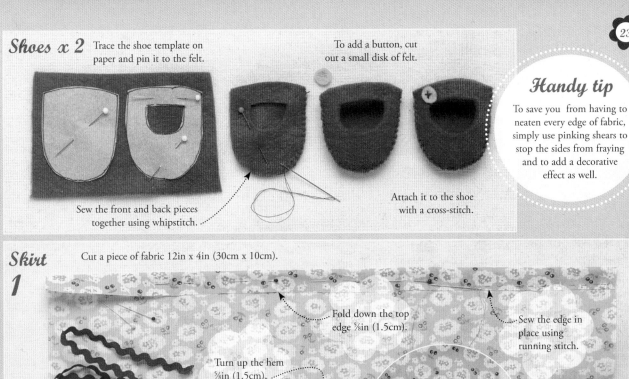

Sew the front and back pieces together using whipstitch.

Attach it to the shoe with a cross-stitch.

Handy tip

To save you from having to neaten every edge of fabric, simply use pinking shears to stop the sides from fraying and to add a decorative effect as well.

Skirt

1

Cut a piece of fabric 12in x 4in (30cm x 10cm).

Fold down the top edge ⅝in (1.5cm).

Sew the edge in place using running stitch.

Turn up the hem ⅝in (1.5cm).

Sew rickrack to the front of the skirt along the hem edge. Use pinking shears to neaten the edge of the fabric.

2

Cut a piece of ribbon 10in (25cm) and fasten a safety pin to one end.

Push the pin into the gap in the fabric and work it through.

Fit the skirt around your doll's waist and tie the ribbon into a bow.

3

Pull the pin out at the other end. Don't pull the ribbon all the way through.

Gather the fabric on the ribbon.

Lottie's brothers

Lottie has two brothers, Billy and Jim. These boys are made from the Lottie doll pattern, too, but they have short, neat hair and little ears.

Find the template for the Lottie doll on pages 13–19.

Jim   Lottie   Billy

Jim's sweater and jeans

Turn to the next page to find out how to make the clothes.

Sweater

The sweater is knitted in four pieces in stockinette stitch. The stripes are knitted in to create a pattern.

Jeans

Made in a lightweight cotton fabric that looks like denim.

Satchel

Shoulder bag made from felt with felt straps.

Shoes

Contrasting felt for the uppers, the soles, and the toes. Finished with a shoelace effect.

You will need

A BASIC DOLL (see pages 14–19) • Sewing kit (see pages 112–113)
SWEATER: • Ball of yarn for the main color, and scraps for stripes
JEANS: • Cotton fabric 6in x 9in (15cm x 22cm), elastic 7in (18cm)
SHOES and BAG: • Scraps of felt in red, gray, and white, and two browns

How to make jeans

Jeans

1

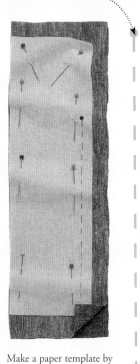

Sew leg seam up to this dot.

FOLD LINE for fabric

Make a paper template by tracing over the lines shown here. Pin the paper to the folded fabric, as shown, and cut it out. Repeat to make a second leg.

2

Using backstitch, sew the inside leg seams together up to the dot.

Mark the dot on the fabric.

Make a left and right leg.

3

Bring the legs together and match up the dots on each leg. Sew the back seam from the dot marker up to the waist.

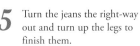

Repeat this for the front seam.

4

Fold over the top of the waistband ⅜in (1cm).

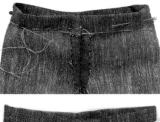

Use running stitch to sew it in place.

Attach a safety pin to the elastic.

Place the pin at the join of the back seam and feed the elastic around the inside of the waist.

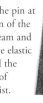

Bring the pin through and gather the material to the required size.

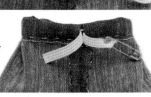

Sew the ends of the elastic together and hide it back into the waistband.

5

Turn the jeans the right-way out and turn up the legs to finish them.

Sweater

FRONT and BACK
Use stockinette stitch.
Cast on 24 stitches.
Rib 6 rows: Row 1: Knit 1,
purl 1, repeat to end.
Repeat row 1 five more times.
Work 21 rows in stockinette
stitch, beginning with a knit row.
Rib 3 rows: Row 1: Knit 1, purl 1,
repeat to end. Repeat row 1 two
more times. Cast off.

SLEEVES x 2
Use stockinette stitch.
Cast on 20 stitches.
Rib 3 rows: Row 1: Knit 1,
purl 1, repeat to end.
Row 2 and 3: Repeat row 1.
Work 11 rows in stockinette stitch,
beginning with a knit row.
Cast off.

3 rows of ribbing

6 rows of ribbing

3 rows of ribbing

1

Place the front and back pieces right-sides down.

Sew along the edges on each side to create the neckline.

Use the loose ends to sew up the edges.

2

Place the right sides together.

Align the center of the sleeve with the neckline and pin the edges together.

Sew the edges together to attach the sleeve to the front and back pieces.

Open the knitting out flat.

Fold the knitting over with the reverse side out.

3

Use the loose ends to sew up the edges.

Sew the edges together up the sides and along the sleeves.

Turn the sweater right-side out and put it on your doll.

Sweater designs

You can change this sweater pattern to create other designs, including stripes, bands, and multicolored yarn for an instant colorful effect.

Shoes

Trace the shoe templates onto paper and pin them to the felt.

Decorate the front first; sew on the toe cap and add the laces.

Using whipstitch, sew the front and back together.

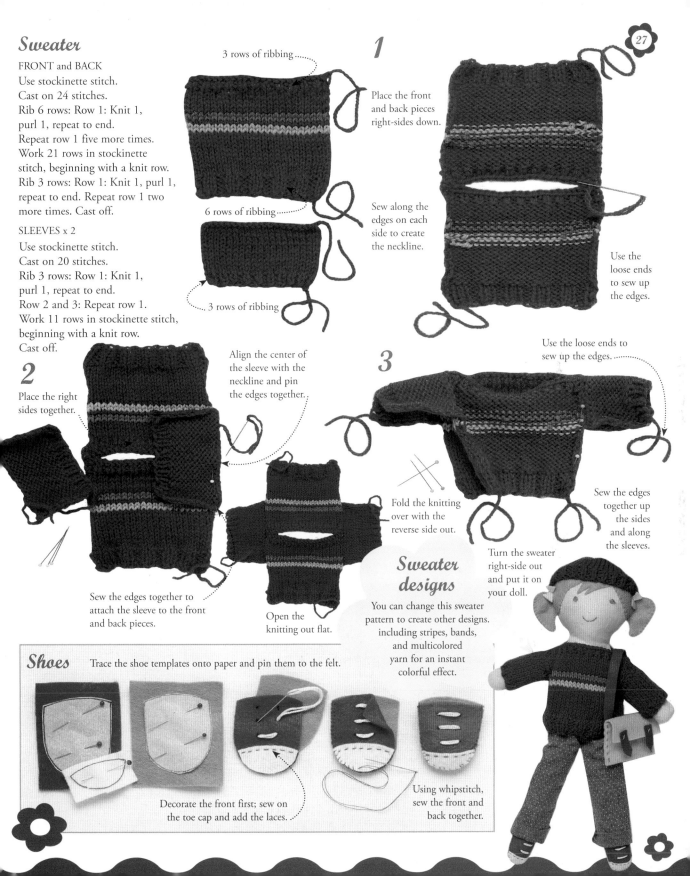

Lottie, Billy, and...

Lottie

Billy

24

Make Lottie's sweater using the pattern for Jim's. Use multicolored yarn to create the pattern.

Lottie's jeans are just the same as Jim's, but hers are made from dotted lightweight cotton fabric.

Billy's sweater is also made using the knitting pattern. Create this two-tone effect by knitting the bottom half in dark blue yarn, then changing to pale blue yarn for the top half and arms.

*They are ready to go out—*Billy has his camera and is set to tal

Jim

Jim

Jim's beanie is simple
to make—just knit a
rectangular shape, sew
the sides together, then
gather the yarn at the top.

For Jim's scarf, simply
knit a length of scarf
long enough to wrap
around his neck.
See pages 32.

Meow,
MEOW!

Woof,
WOOF!

Jim is walking his dog, who's just spied a cat in the window!

Make accessories for your dolls

Beanie hats

Wool scarf

Multicolored yarn creates a striped effect.

Shoulder bags

Make bags in different colors to match outfits.

Camera

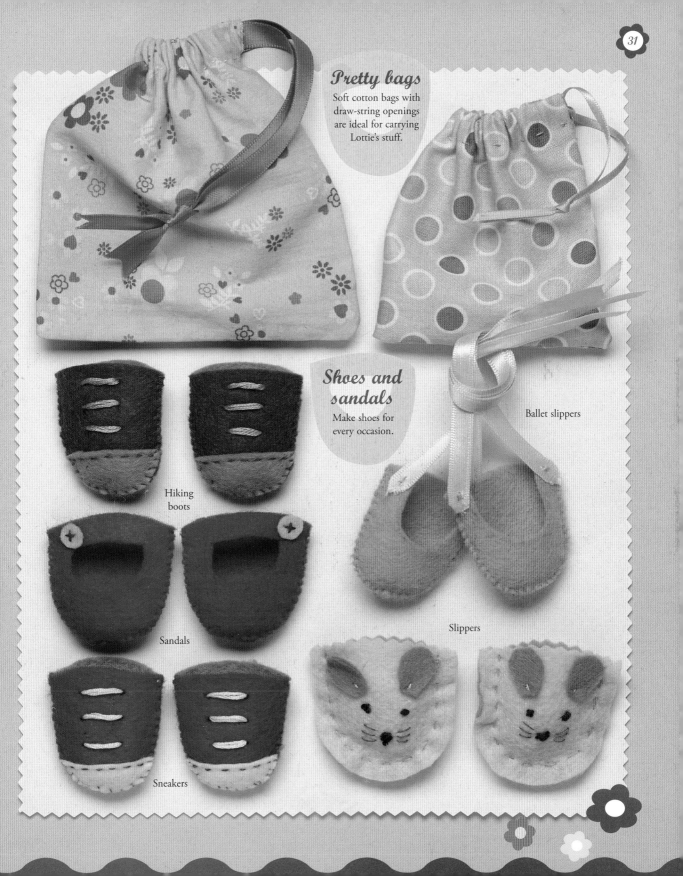

Pretty bags

Soft cotton bags with draw-string openings are ideal for carrying Lottie's stuff.

Shoes and sandals

Make shoes for every occasion.

Ballet slippers

Hiking boots

Sandals

Slippers

Sneakers

How to make accessories

Camera

Black yarn for strap

Scraps of black and gray felt

Cutout felt shapes.

For front and back 1in x 1¾in (2.5cm x 4cm).

Decorative strips ¼in x 1¾in (6mm x 4cm) for and small disks for lens.

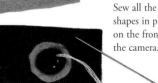

Sew all the shapes in place on the front of the camera.

Sew the front camera piece to the back.

Stitch the end of the thread to the back of the camera.

Wool scarf

Cast on more stitches to make a wider scarf.

Cast on 8 stitches. In knit stitch, work rows until the scarf is as long as you like.

Shoe bag

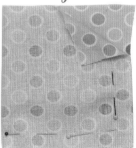

Cut a piece of fabric 7in x 4in (17cm x 10 cm) and fold it in half, with right sides facing.

Pin along the bottom and side. Sew together.

Fold over the top edge ½in (13mm), pin, and stitch.

Pull the ribbon through the fold using a safety pin attached to the end.

Turn the bag right-side out. Pull the ribbon to gather the opening.

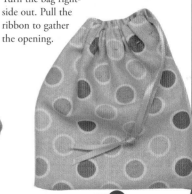

Beanie hat

Cast on 48 stitches.
Rib stitch 5 rows.
Row 1: Knit 1,
purl 1 to end.
Repeat 4 more rows.
Work 10 rows in
stockinette stitch.
Cast off.

Pull the yarn to gather
the knitting. Secure
the yarn to finish.

Fold the work
in half, right
sides together.

Sew the side
seam together.

Sew around the top
edge of the knitting.

Satchel bag

Cut out the felt.
Buckle straps:
½in x 1½in
(13mm x
3.8cm). Bag
straps: ½in x
4½in (1.3cm x
11.5cm) and ½in
x 3in (1.3cm x
7.6cm).

Felt for the bag:
3⅛in x 7in
(8cm x 18cm)

Fold
over the
bottom
third of
the felt.

Sew in
place.

Sew the
straps
together.

Attach the
buckle straps
to the front
of the
bag and
sew
in place.

Sew the
ends of
the straps
to the
back of
the bag.

Ballerinas

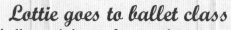

Lottie goes to ballet class

The ballerinas' dainty feet are always on tiptoe.
Their frilly skirts are made from netting fabric
gathered to create the perfect tutu effect.

Find the pattern
for the Lottie doll on pages 14–19.

Ballerina tutu and shoes

See the next page to find out how to make the clothes.

Leotard

A felt bodice with ribbon shoulder straps held at the back with a safety pin and a ribbon waistband.

Tutu

A frothy skirt made with layers of netting fabric gathered with a ribbon and tied at the back.

Ballet shoes

Dancing shoes made from felt with ribbon ties.

You will need

A BASIC DOLL (see pages 14–19) • Sewing kit (see pages 112–113)
TUTU: 3 pieces of netting fabric 7½in x 27½in (19cm x 70cm)
• Ribbon 16in (40cm) in length
LEOTARD: Felt 7in x 5in (18cm x 13cm) • 2 lengths of ribbon 4in (10cm)
for shoulder straps • 8in (20cm) for waistband • 2 small safety pins.
SHOES: Scraps of pink felt • 4 lengths of ribbon 8in (20cm).

How to dress a ballerina

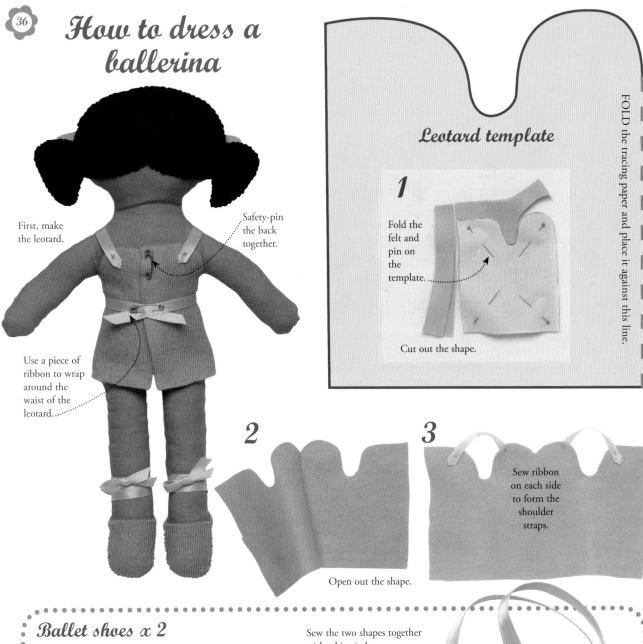

First, make the leotard.

Safety-pin the back together.

Use a piece of ribbon to wrap around the waist of the leotard.

Leotard template

1
Fold the felt and pin on the template.

Cut out the shape.

FOLD the tracing paper and place it against this line.

2
Open out the shape.

3
Sew ribbon on each side to form the shoulder straps.

Ballet shoes x 2

Trace the ballet shoe templates on page 14 onto paper and cut them out of the felt.

Sew the two shapes together with whipstitch.

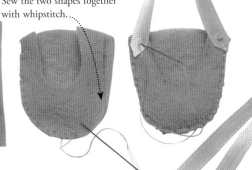

Sew the ribbon to each side of the shoe.

Tutu

Place the three pieces of netting on top of each other. Fold the whole stack over lengthwise to make one long strip.

Sew along the fold ½in (12mm) from the edge.

Pin a safety pin to one end of the ribbon. Work the pin along the gap in the netting.

Bring the pin through to the other end, gather the fabric, and tie around the waist.

Fairy wings

A pair of sparkly wings will transform your ballerina doll into a flying fairy. Use pretty ribbons to attach wings at her shoulders.

1

Pin the template to the felt. Cut two wing shapes.

2

BACK WINGS

FRONT WINGS

Buttons and ribbons

...... Draw where the ribbons will be positioned.

Wings Cut 2

Fold a piece of tracing paper in half. Place it against the fold line and trace over the outline.

FOLD the tracing paper and place it against this line.

3

Sew on the ribbons and buttons.

4

Pin the felt pieces together. Use running stitch to sew.

Embroidery thread..........

5

Cut two lengths of ribbon 8in (20cm) long.

Sew the ribbon ties in position on the back of the wings.

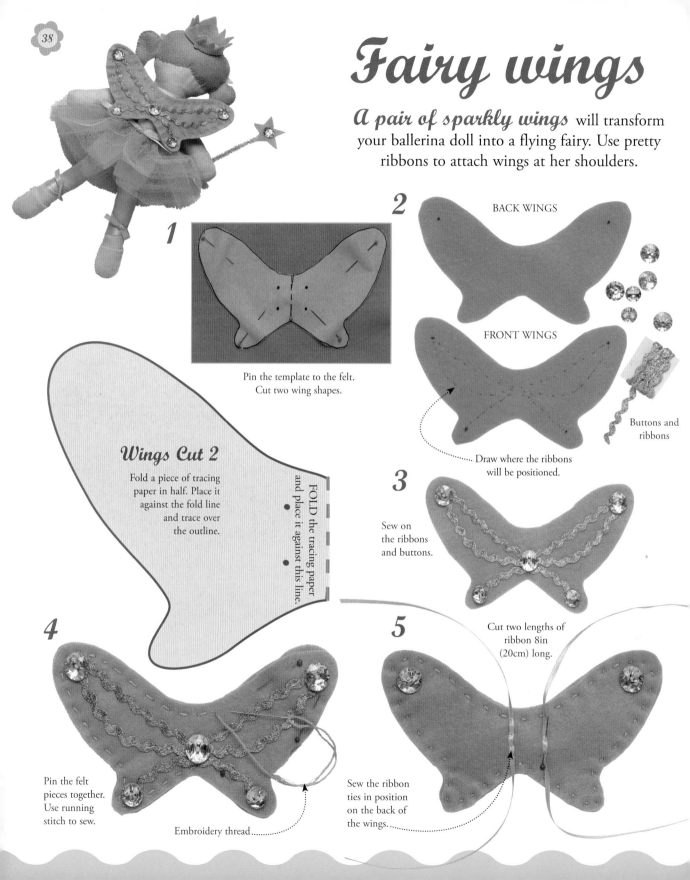

For wings
You will need

- Sewing kit (see pages 112–113)
- Felt fabric
- Buttons and ribbon for decoration
- Ribbon to attach wings
- Felt-tip marker

Crown

Cut a felt strip long enough to fit around the top of your fairy's head. Shape the top; wrap the felt around; secure with a stitch at the back.

Wand

Cut a star from a scrap of felt. Sew a glittery button to the center. Attach the star to a pipe cleaner.

Nighttime

Feeling tired? Lottie and Baby Lottie are ready for bed.

Baby Lottie doll

Make a baby doll to match Lottie. She has a felt body and a soft cotton nightie. Find the pattern on page 100.

Find the template
for the Lottie doll on pages 14–19.

Pajamas and slippers

See the next page to find out how to make clothes.

Pajamas

Make a simple pajama top gathered at the neck with ribbon.

Pretty bag

Baby Lottie doll

See page 100 to make doll.

The bottoms are baggy pants made from soft cotton fabric.

Slippers

No nightwear is complete without extra-comfy slippers.

You will need

A BASIC DOLL (see pages 13–19) • Sewing kit (see pages 112–113)
PAJAMAS: Cotton fabric for pajama top 10in x 6in (25cm x 15cm)
and bottoms 11in x 11in (28cm x 28cm). Elastic 7in (40cm) • Ribbon 12in (30cm)
SLIPPERS: Scraps of pink, blue, and gray felt.

How to make night clothes

Pajama bottoms

2 Using backstitch, sew the inside leg seams together up to the dot.

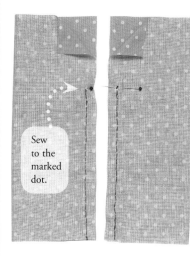

Sew to the marked dot.

3 Bring the legs together and match up the dots on each leg.

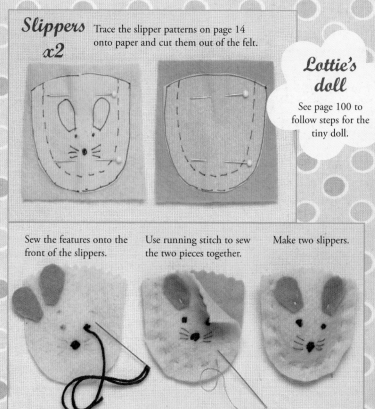

Sew the back seam together from the dot marker up to the waist. Repeat for the front seam.

This dot shows where to stop sewing when you sew the leg seams. Mark it on your fabric...

1

FOLD LINE for fabric

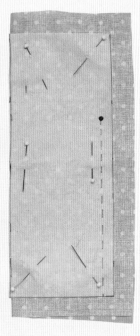

Make a paper template by tracing over the lines shown here. Pin the paper to the fabric, which should be folded right-sides together. Cut out.

Pajama bottoms template Cut 2

Slippers x2

Trace the slipper patterns on page 14 onto paper and cut them out of the felt.

Lottie's doll

See page 100 to follow steps for the tiny doll.

Sew the features onto the front of the slippers.

Use running stitch to sew the two pieces together.

Make two slippers.

4 Fold over the top of the waistline ½in (12mm).

Use running stitch to sew it in place.

Attach a safety pin to the elastic.

Starting at the join of the back seam, feed the elastic around the inside of the waist hem.

Bring the pin through and gather the material to the required size.

Sew the ends of the elastic together and hide it back into the waistband.

5 Turn the bottoms right-side out, then turn up the legs. Sew them to finish.

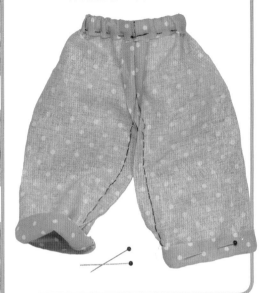

Nightie Cut a piece of fabric 10in x 4in (25cm x 10cm).

1 Trim the sides with pinking shears.

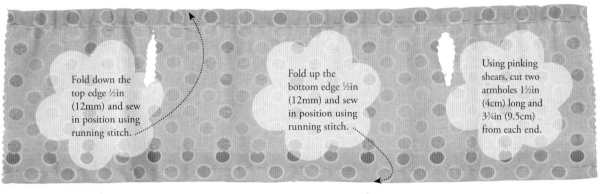

Fold down the top edge ½in (12mm) and sew in position using running stitch.

Fold up the bottom edge ½in (12mm) and sew in position using running stitch.

Using pinking shears, cut two armholes 1½in (4cm) long and 3¾in (9.5cm) from each end.

2 Attach a safety pin to one end of the ribbon.

Work the ribbon through the hem at the neck.

3 Bring the ribbon through to the other side, gather the fabric, and tie.

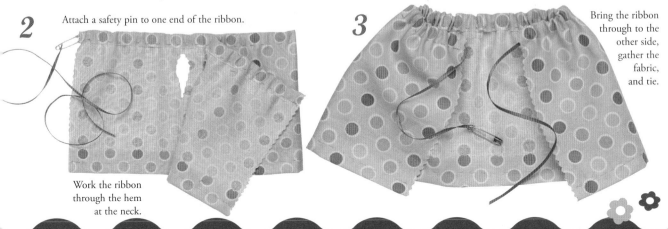

Lottie's mix-and-match wardrobe

I'm wrapped up to go out in the cold!

That hat with this bag, or this skirt with that sweater? The possibitities are endless!

Shelly the Mermaid

Strands of colorful yarn are perfect for Shelly's hair.

Chunky yarns give a seaweed effect.

Swishing hair and fishy tails

To make a mermaid, use the Lottie doll pattern on page 14 for her upper body, head, and arms. Then follow the template shown here for her lower body and tail.

Part *a*

Mark these big dots on the fabric. They indicate where to stop sewing and leave an opening for the mermaid's body.

How to make...

A PAPER TEMPLATE FROM THIS TEMPLATE.
Trace pattern "b" then move it over. Align it with the top of template "a" and continue tracing around the shape to make one outline. Follow Step 1 instructions on the next page.

Template for mermaid's tail

You will need

Materials for a BASIC DOLL (see pages 14–17)
• Sewing kit (see pages 112–113)
TAIL: Cotton fabric 16in x 12in (40cm x 30cm)
• Poly fill
HAIR: Balls of different colored yarn • Felt
• Thick cardboard 20in x 4in (50cm x 10cm)
DECORATION: Ribbon, button, and felt

Part *b*

These "V" shapes show where to snip the fabric to help shape the doll.

DOTTED LINE shows where to sew your project.

Find the template

for Lottie doll on pages 14–19.

How to make Shelly the Mermaid

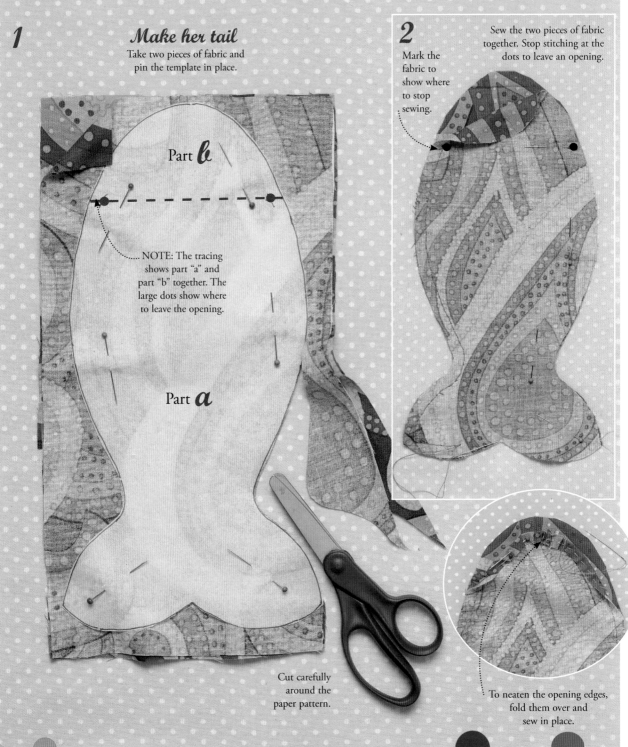

1 ### Make her tail
Take two pieces of fabric and pin the template in place.

Part **b**

NOTE: The tracing shows part "a" and part "b" together. The large dots show where to leave the opening.

Part **a**

Cut carefully around the paper pattern.

2

Mark the fabric to show where to stop sewing.

Sew the two pieces of fabric together. Stop stitching at the dots to leave an opening.

To neaten the opening edges, fold them over and sew in place.

Make her body and sew it to her tail

Make the upper body as shown on pages 14–17.

NOTE: The mermaid's body is shorter than Lottie's.

Fill the upper body. Don't overfill or it will be difficult to attach to the tail.

Fill the tail—again, don't overfill.

1 Place the upper body inside the tail and work it into position.

2 Pin the tail to the body, front, back, and sides.

3 Sew the tail neatly and securely to the body all the way around.

Now it's time to add Shelly's hair.

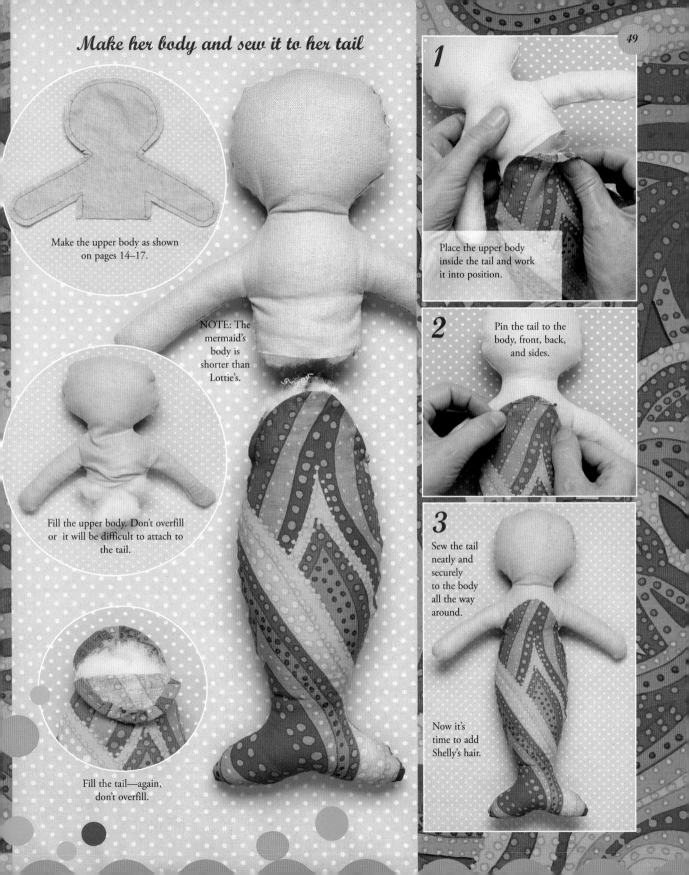

1 Start her hair

Pin the hair base patterns to the felt and cut them out.

2

Place the base on to the head and work it into position.

NOTE: Use the template on page 15 for the base shape and follow the instructions on page 18 for how to make it.

3

Sew the base neatly in place all the way around the head.

4 Make her hair

Wrap yarn around a piece of thick card. Wind each color about four times.

Pull the yarn off the cardboard carefully and tie it up tightly in the middle.

Cut a length of yarn for tying.

Cardboard 20in x 4in (50cm x 10cm).

5

Cut another length of yarn and stitch the tresses to her head.

Bring the needle up through the bunch of yarn.

Knot the end of the yarn and bring the needle through.

6

Bring the yarn backward and forward through the bunch of yarn and tie it off securely.

7 Tie each side of her hair into bunches and attach to the sides of her head with yarn.

Tie the yarn into a bow.

Pull the yarn half way through.

Tiny beads add a glint to her eye.

Sew on a button.

Sew ribbon, such as rickrack, around her waist.

Make her face

For her eyes, cut small disks of felt and stitch them in place. Make eye lashes with stitches coming out from her eyes. Her mouth is made up of tiny stitches.

Leave the ends of her hair as they are—the more ragged the hair, the more it looks like seaweed.

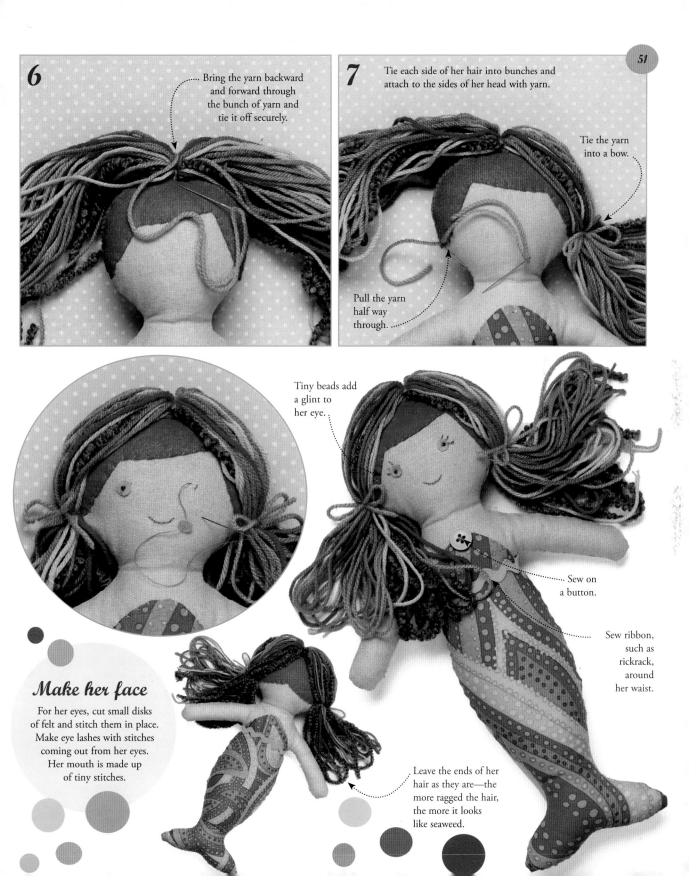

Cinders

Lucky Cinders!
From her dreary, drab work clothes, she's magically transformed into a glamorous princess ready for the ball. It's a topsy-turvy world for this doll.

Cinderella

She will go to the ball!

How to make Cinders / Cinderella

This topsy-turvy doll has one body with a head on both ends and four arms. Finish the body and attach the bodice fabric, then sew on the arms.

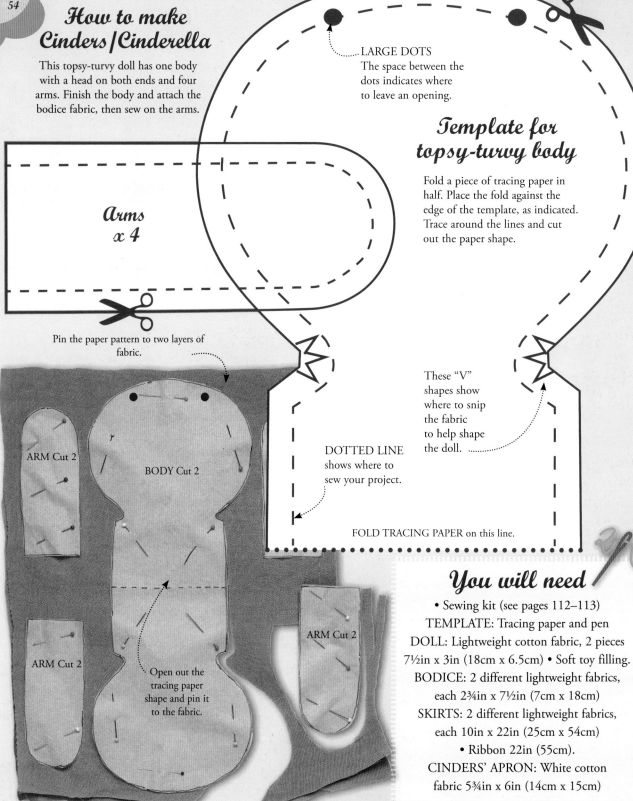

Arms x 4

Pin the paper pattern to two layers of fabric.

LARGE DOTS
The space between the dots indicates where to leave an opening.

Template for topsy-turvy body

Fold a piece of tracing paper in half. Place the fold against the edge of the template, as indicated. Trace around the lines and cut out the paper shape.

These "V" shapes show where to snip the fabric to help shape the doll.

DOTTED LINE shows where to sew your project.

FOLD TRACING PAPER on this line.

ARM Cut 2

BODY Cut 2

ARM Cut 2

ARM Cut 2

Open out the tracing paper shape and pin it to the fabric.

You will need

• Sewing kit (see pages 112–113)
TEMPLATE: Tracing paper and pen
DOLL: Lightweight cotton fabric, 2 pieces 7½in x 3in (18cm x 6.5cm) • Soft toy filling.
BODICE: 2 different lightweight fabrics, each 2¾in x 7½in (7cm x 18cm)
SKIRTS: 2 different lightweight fabrics, each 10in x 22in (25cm x 54cm)
• Ribbon 22in (55cm).
CINDERS' APRON: White cotton fabric 5¾in x 6in (14cm x 15cm)

Make the body

1 Using backstitch, sew all the way around the body shape.

2

...Leave an opening for the filling.

Turn the body shape right-side out and fill evenly.

Fold the edges over and sew up the opening.

Make four arms

1 With right sides together, sew around the two arm pieces; leave the end open.

2 Turn the arm inside out and fill.

NOTE: Only fill the arm halfway.

3 Fold the ends in and pin them together.

4 Neatly sew the opening closed.

Dress bodice

1 Fold over the fabric edge ½in (1cm) and sew it in place.

Cut two pieces of fabric 2¾in x 7in (7cm x 18cm).

2 Place the fabrics together with right sides facing. Pin in place.

Sew the two pieces together using running stitch.

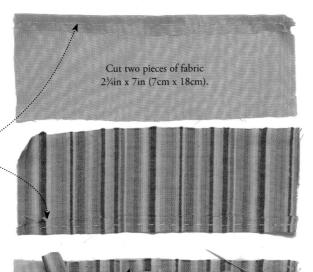

3 Open out the fabric. Fold the edge over and sew it down.

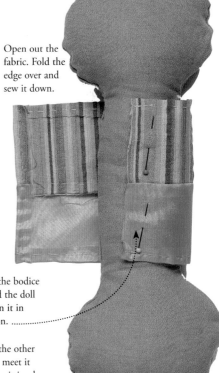

Wrap the bodice around the doll and pin it in position.

Bring the other end to meet it and sew it in place.

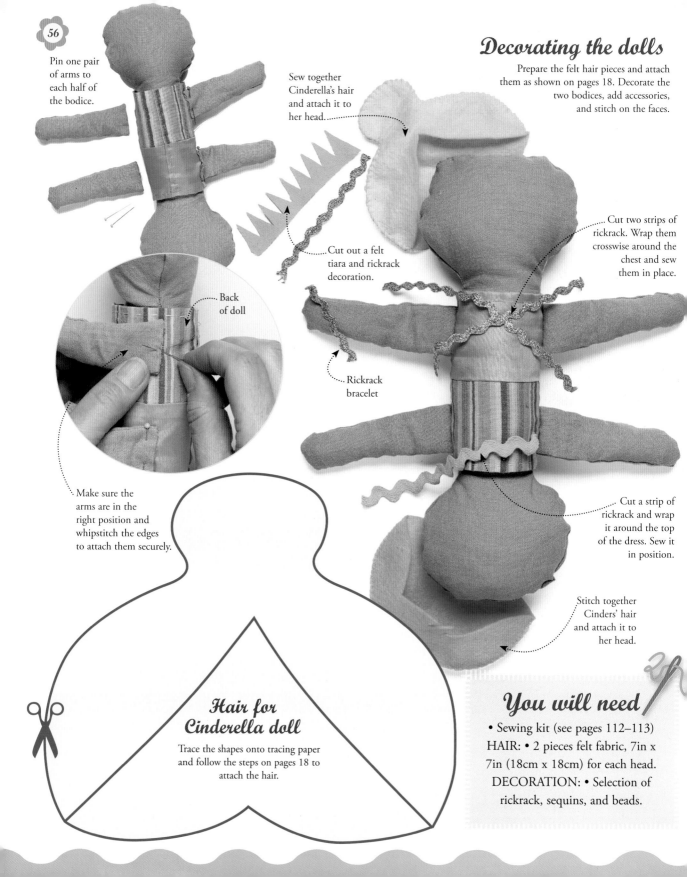

Pin one pair of arms to each half of the bodice.

Decorating the dolls

Prepare the felt hair pieces and attach them as shown on pages 18. Decorate the two bodices, add accessories, and stitch on the faces.

Sew together Cinderella's hair and attach it to her head.

Cut out a felt tiara and rickrack decoration.

Cut two strips of rickrack. Wrap them crosswise around the chest and sew them in place.

Back of doll

Rickrack bracelet

Make sure the arms are in the right position and whipstitch the edges to attach them securely.

Cut a strip of rickrack and wrap it around the top of the dress. Sew it in position.

Stitch together Cinders' hair and attach it to her head.

Hair for Cinderella doll

Trace the shapes onto tracing paper and follow the steps on pages 18 to attach the hair.

You will need

• Sewing kit (see pages 112–113)
HAIR: • 2 pieces felt fabric, 7in x 7in (18cm x 18cm) for each head.
DECORATION: • Selection of rickrack, sequins, and beads.

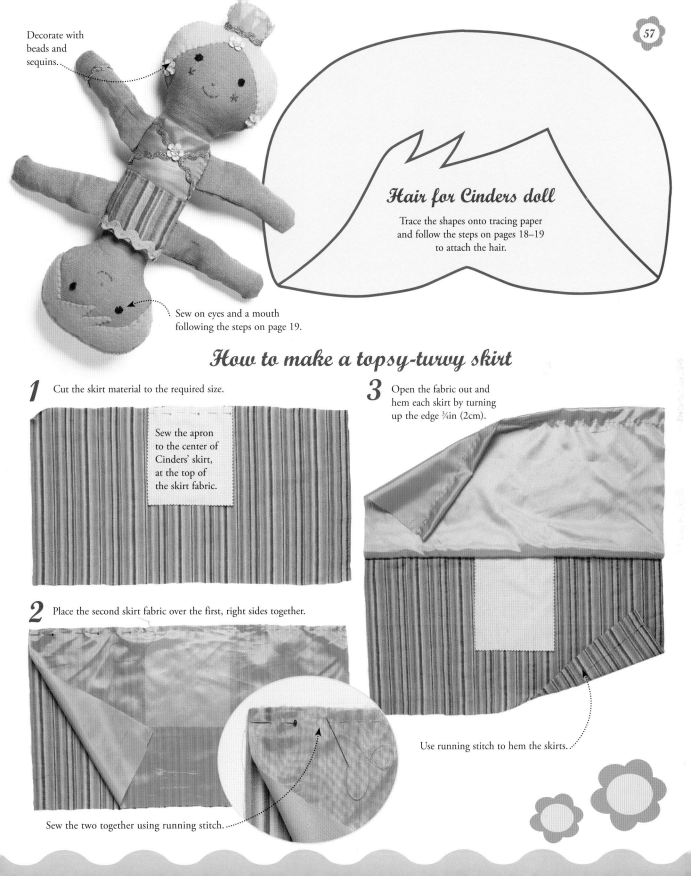

Decorate with beads and sequins.

Sew on eyes and a mouth following the steps on page 19.

Hair for Cinders doll

Trace the shapes onto tracing paper and follow the steps on pages 18–19 to attach the hair.

How to make a topsy-turvy skirt

1 Cut the skirt material to the required size.

Sew the apron to the center of Cinders' skirt, at the top of the skirt fabric.

2 Place the second skirt fabric over the first, right sides together.

Sew the two together using running stitch.

3 Open the fabric out and hem each skirt by turning up the edge ¾in (2cm).

Use running stitch to hem the skirts.

4

Fold the fabric over so the right sides are facing.

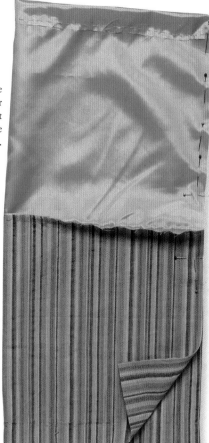

5

Pin and sew the sides together using backstitch.

Stop 2½in (6cm) from the seam on each side.

Finish the seams and bring one skirt over the other so Cinders' skirt is facing out.

6

Fold neatly at the seam and pin around the top of the skirt.

Using running stitch, sew around the top of the skirt ½in (12mm) from the top.

7

Attach a safety pin to one end of the ribbon.

Feed the pin into the opening and work it all the way through.

Pull the ribbon through, then remove the pin and gather the skirt.

Sew rickrack around the bottom edge of Cinders' skirt and add a patch to the apron.

Finishing the doll

Handy tip

Tie the ribbon tightly around the waist. To prevent the skirt from slipping up and down, add a few stitches to anchor the top of the skirt to the waistline.

Add rickrack and other decorations to Cinderella's skirt.

Place the skirt on the waistline and arrange the gathers.

Place the doll inside the skirt, gather it, and tie the ribbon into a bow.

Wake up, and...

Sleepy or wide awake? Here's a simple alternative for a topsy-turvy doll.

Position the skirt at the waistline, then sew it to the bodice fabric.

To make your doll

Follow the steps for Cinders/Cinderella on the previous pages. Choose different patterned fabric for the nightgown and day dress. The hair is made using the template on page 15; for the face, see page 19.

... rise and shine

Pillow and nightie

Make a pillow from leftover nightgown fabric.

Day dress

2

Yarn
dolls

Go knit yourself

Make a doll that looks like you. Simply follow this knitting pattern to create your own doll. The colored stripes will make up the parts of the body.

"Hi, I'm Jane Bull."

Yarn for skin

Yarn for top

Yarn for shorts

Yarn for shoes

Hey! You will need

- Sewing kit (see pages 112–113)
- Knitting needles US6 (4mm) • Stitch holder
- Balls of DK weight yarn:
1 ball for skin color • 1 ball for top
1 ball for shorts • 1 ball for shoes
1 ball for hair • Tapestry needle
- Poly fill

You choose how you want your doll to look by changing the colors of the stripes you knit.

Don't change colors— knit an all-in-one.

Ring the changes with bands of color.

Scarlet

Cherry

Sarah

How to make a knitted doll

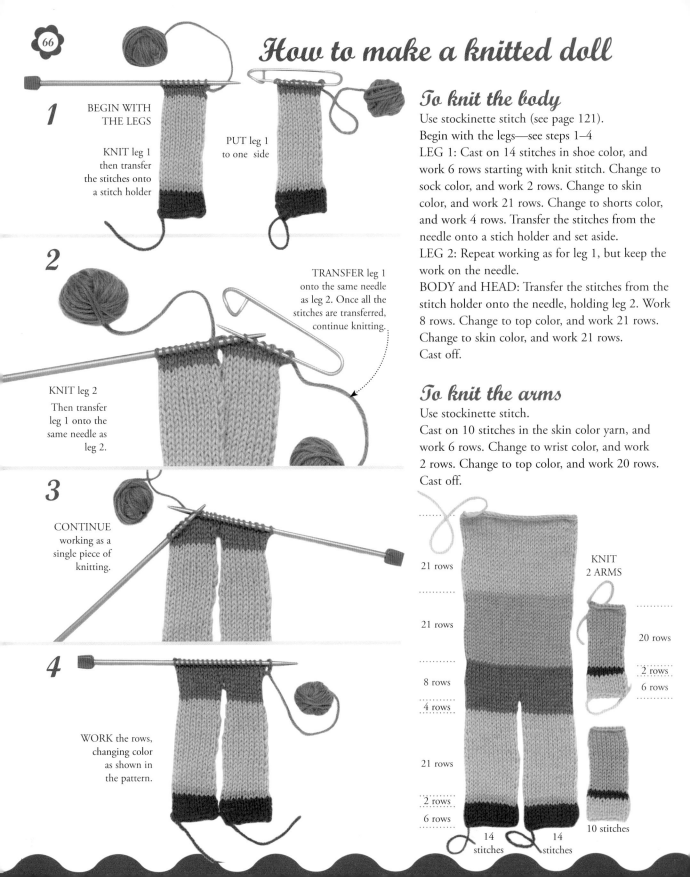

1 BEGIN WITH THE LEGS

KNIT leg 1 then transfer the stitches onto a stitch holder

PUT leg 1 to one side

2 KNIT leg 2

Then transfer leg 1 onto the same needle as leg 2.

TRANSFER leg 1 onto the same needle as leg 2. Once all the stitches are transferred, continue knitting.

3 CONTINUE working as a single piece of knitting.

4 WORK the rows, changing color as shown in the pattern.

To knit the body

Use stockinette stitch (see page 121).
Begin with the legs—see steps 1–4
LEG 1: Cast on 14 stitches in shoe color, and work 6 rows starting with knit stitch. Change to sock color, and work 2 rows. Change to skin color, and work 21 rows. Change to shorts color, and work 4 rows. Transfer the stitches from the needle onto a stich holder and set aside.
LEG 2: Repeat working as for leg 1, but keep the work on the needle.
BODY and HEAD: Transfer the stitches from the stitch holder onto the needle, holding leg 2. Work 8 rows. Change to top color, and work 21 rows. Change to skin color, and work 21 rows. Cast off.

To knit the arms

Use stockinette stitch.
Cast on 10 stitches in the skin color yarn, and work 6 rows. Change to wrist color, and work 2 rows. Change to top color, and work 20 rows. Cast off.

21 rows

21 rows

8 rows

4 rows

21 rows

2 rows

6 rows

14 stitches   14 stitches

KNIT 2 ARMS

20 rows

2 rows

6 rows

10 stitches

Finish the body

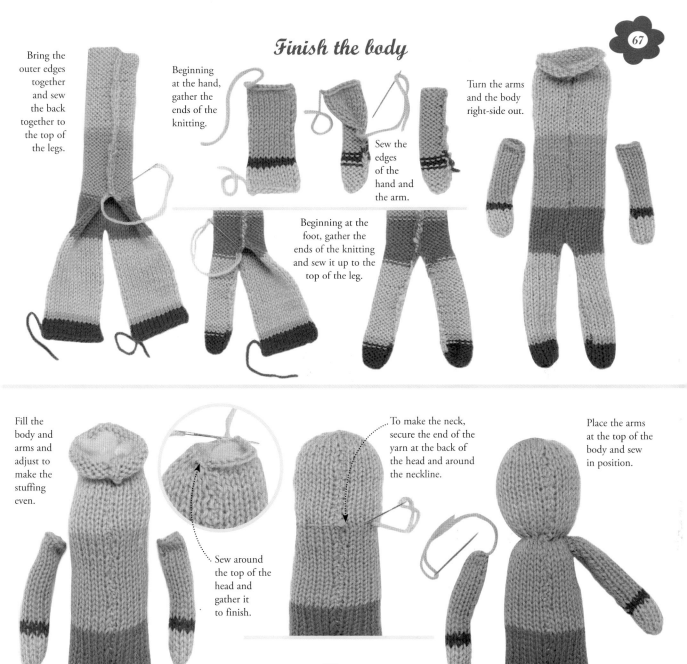

Bring the outer edges together and sew the back together to the top of the legs.

Beginning at the hand, gather the ends of the knitting.

Sew the edges of the hand and the arm.

Turn the arms and the body right-side out.

Beginning at the foot, gather the ends of the knitting and sew it up to the top of the leg.

Fill the body and arms and adjust to make the stuffing even.

Sew around the top of the head and gather it to finish.

To make the neck, secure the end of the yarn at the back of the head and around the neckline.

Place the arms at the top of the body and sew in position.

Pull the yarn to form a tight head shape. Fasten off the yarn securely.

For hair, ears, and eyes you will need

- Sewing kit (see pages 112–113)
- Tapestry needle
- Ball of hair-colored yarn
- Cardboard 9in x 3in (22cm x 8cm)
- Short lengths of yarn for ears, eyes, and mouth

Use blanket stitch to make the ears.

How to make hair

1

Cardboard

Yarn for hair

Carefully take the yarn off the cardboard.

Cut a length of yarn and place it around the middle of the bundle.

Tie the yarn tightly and make a knot.

Wrap the yarn around the cardboard 30 times.

2

Position the bundle over the center of the head.

3

Thread yarn through a needle, knot the end, and pull the needle through the top of the head.

Put the needle through the middle of the hair and secure tightly to the head.

Bring the needle in to the head and out through the hair three times. Tie off.

...and bangs

Thread yarn through a needle, and knot the end. Put the needle in under the hair, then make log stitches to create bangs.

Start the bangs at the side of the head.

How to make ears

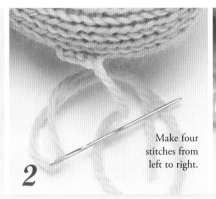

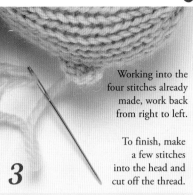

1 Thread a length of yarn on the needle and knot the end. Put the yarn into the side of the head and make a stitch.

2 Make four stitches from left to right.

3 Working into the four stitches already made, work back from right to left.

To finish, make a few stitches into the head and cut off the thread.

How to make a face

Decide what kind of face your doll will have. Use wool yarn to make the features.

1 Bring the yarn through the back of the head.

Use backstitch to sew the mouth shape.

2 Bring the yarn back to the side of the head. Snip off the yarn and the knot.

Repeat Steps 1 and 2 for the eyes.

TIP FOR SEWING FEATURES
To hide the end of the thread, first knot the end of the yarn and bring it through the side of the head and out to the front in the position where the mouth will be. Sew the mouth shape, then bring the yarn back through to the side of the head. Snip off the yarn and the knot.

Bags and beads

To knit a bag

Use stockinette stitch (see page 121).
Cast on 20 stitches.
Work 32 rows in the main color.
Cast off.

FOR THE HANDLES: See page 123.
Make 34 chain stitches. Leave the strands
on both ends to sew to the bag.

1 Fold the rectangle in half, with the right sides facing in.

Sew down both the edges.

2 Sew the handles to each side of the bag.

The handles are made of a foundation
chain using a crochet hook
(see page 123).

You can make larger bags by
increasing the number of
stitches and rows you use.

To knit a skirt

Use stockinette stitch (see page 121).
Cast on 60 stitches.
Work 22 rows in the main color,
beginning with a knit row.
Row 23: Knit 2 together, knit 1.
Repeat to end. (40 stitches remain).
Row 24: Purl to end.
Row 25: Knit 2, knit 2 together.
Repeat to end. (30 stitches remain).
Row 26: Purl to end.
Row 27 and 28: Knit and purl row
in the contrasting color.
Note: Don't cut off the main color;
leave it until it's needed again.
Row 29: Knit in the main color
to the end.
Cast off.

Your knitting
should flare out,
as shown here.

Leave the loose ends
and use them to sew
the skirt together.

Fold the knitting in half,
with the right sides
facing in. Sew the
sides together.

The finished
skirt is ready
to go!

To make a necklace

Using a needle and thread, tie a knot around one of the beads.

Thread the beads onto the thread.

Threading complete

Pass the needle back through the first bead a few times and make a knot.

Attach the necklace by sewing in and out of the doll and the necklace. Secure the thread, then trim it.

Hairstyles

Make a neat style by tying the hair into pigtails. Sew a length of yarn on each side of the head and tie it around the hair in a bow. Your doll can also wear her hair up in a bun.

Add beads for earrings.

Skirts and bags

Experiment with the design of the skirt to suit your doll. Here's a fancy one that has the pattern knitted into it. To design this pattern, change the color of the yarn as you knit, making stitches in different colors to create a patterned effect.

Make mini-knitting

Complete the look for your dolls with tiny knitting needles and yarn. Take two wooden toothpicks and glue a bead to the end of each. Then, to make the knitting, cast on as usual and start knitting!

Pirate Pete

How to make pirates and heroes

These dolls are made using the same method used to make the dolls on pages 64–68. Work with the yarn colors shown here or choose your own color scheme.

For his ears, follow the steps on pages 68–69.

Use black yarn to sew an eye patch and black felt for his mustache.

His earrings are loops of gold thread sewn to his ears.

To make a rolled-up pants effect, knit stitch the first row of the pants then knit, purl, and knit the next three rows. This will give a raised effect to the front of the work. Continue to work in stockinette stitch.

For his gold belt, sew a buckle shape using gold thread.

You will need

- Colorful yarn
- US6 (4mm) knitting needles
- Tapestry needle
- Poly fill
- Sewing kit (see pages 112–113)

To knit the body

Use stockinette stitch (see page 121). Begin with the legs. LEG 1: Cast on 14 stitches. BOOTS: Work 12 rows, beginning with knit stitch. PANTS: Work 22 rows in brown, transfer stitches to stitch holder. LEG 2: Repeat as for leg 1. BODY: Put stitches on one needle and continue pants. Work 9 rows. BELT: Work 3 rows in black. SHIRT: Work 14 rows in stripes, two rows per white and blue stripe. HEAD: Work 13 rows in flesh color. HAT: Work 8 rows in red. Cast off.

To knit the arms

Use stockinette stitch (see page 121). Cast on 10 stitches. HANDS: Work 6 rows in flesh colour. SHIRT SLEEVES: Work 20 rows in stripes of two rows for each color, white and blue. Cast off.

Superhero

To knit the body

Use stockinette stitch (see page 121). Begin with the legs. LEG 1: Cast on 14 stitches in purple. BOOTS: Work 12 rows, beginning with knit stitch. Work 2 rows in blue stripe. PANTS: Work 22 rows, then transfer stitches to stitch holder. LEG 2: Repeat as for leg 1. BODY: Place stitches onto one needle and change to color for shorts, and work 9 rows. BELT: Work 3 rows in purple. SHIRT: Work 15 rows in yellow. HEAD: Work 8 rows in flesh color, 4 rows in purple, and 1 row in blue. HAT: Work 8 rows in yellow. Cast off.

To knit the arms

Use stockinette stitch (see page 121). Cast on 10 stitches. HANDS: Work 6 rows. SHIRT SLEEVES: Work 20 rows. Make one stripe in blue, then work 19 rows in yellow. Cast off.

To knit a cape

Use stockinette stitch (see page 121).
Cast on 60 stitches.
Work 22 rows in main color, beginning with a knit row.
Row 23: Knit 2 together, knit 1. Repeat to end. (40 stitches remain.)
Row 24: Purl to end.
Row 25: Knit 2, knit 2 together. Repeat to end. (30 stitches remain.)
Row 26: Purl to end.
Work 3 more rows.
Cast off.

To attach the cape, sew it to the back of the head at the neckline.

Make three stitches for his Superhero "S" symbol.

Sew a cross-stitch for his buckle.

The Gloveables

Turn unwanted gloves into loveable characters.
Here, Daisy Doll shows off her petal hair,
flared skirt, and sassy boots.

Little
Baby

Mister
Orange

Daisy
Doll

You will need

- A selection of odd gloves
- Poly fill • Sewing kit (see pages 112–113)
- Yarn for features
- Buttons for eyes

TOP: Fingertips form petals and ears.

Cut off the middle finger and thumb to use for the arms.

1 Turn the gloves inside out. Sew the the finger and thumb holes closed, as shown.

2 Turn the gloves right-side out.

Fill the head to make a firm ball shape.

Fill the body and arms.

3

TOP TIP: If the gloves are too long, cut off part of the cuff for a better fit.

Sew around the bottom of the head, gather it tightly, and secure in place.

Cut off the excess from the cuff and keep it for Daisy's skirt.

4 Attach the head to the body. Tuck the head into the top of the other glove and pin in position.

Sew the ends of the arms closed.

5 Sew the arms in position on the sides of the body.

6 Arrange fingertips around the head.

Sew the petals in position from the back.

7 Use yarn for the eyebrows, nose, and mouth.

Use buttons for the eyes.

Daisy's skirt and boots

Use the cuff from the "head" glove to make a waistband.

Spare fingers from other gloves make the skirt.

To make the skirt, choose nine fingers from your collection of gloves and sew them neatly to the underside of the waistband.

For Daisy's boots, use two leftover fingers.

Other Glovables

Little Baby is simply made from two matching gloves using the same method as for Daisy Doll. Just add ears, a button at the belly, and a few strands of yarn for the hair. Give Orange Man a turtleneck sweater by leaving the cuff on the glove body. Sew his hair using black yarn and make a wool hat from the cuff of another glove.

For his turtleneck, leave the cuff of the body glove attached.

Sew on a belly button.

Tiny folks

Knitting tiny people can be a bit tricky, but fun.
They are a great way to use up scraps of yarn.

1 BODY

Work in stockinette stitch (see page 121). Cast on 12 stitches, and work 13 rows for the body and 8 rows for the head.

2 Use the loose end of yarn to gather the top of the head.

Fold the knitting in half, right-sides together. Sew the edges.

Turn the knitting right-side out and fill it.

3 Wrap yarn around the neck to make a head shape.

ARMS and LEGS

For the arms and legs, work in stockinette stitch. For the arms: Cast on 4 stitches, work 9 rows, and cast off. For the legs: Cast on 4 stitches, work 12 rows, and cast off.

Use the ends of the yarn to attach the limbs to the body.

4 Finished and ready to decorate.

Sew the loose end back into the limb to tuck it away.

Place each limb in position against the body and sew it in place.

For long hair, gather the strands of yarn and fasten them to the center of the head.

To make hair, use yarn and sew short and long stitches from the center of the head outward.

The dolls can have rounded bodies. Simply gather in the same way as for the head.

Use yarn to make the eyes and mouth.

Make a brooch

To turn one of your tiny dolls into a brooch, just sew a safety pin to the back and you've made a brooch!

Tiny variations

Be creative—make your folks bigger by casting on more stitches and adding more rows. Do the same for longer or shorter limbs.

Sew in and out around the waist to make a belt.

The good, the bad, and the cuddly

This clutch of characters is easy to make. Simply knit some striped square shapes, sew them up, and add filling to make them soft and cuddly. Even the baddies are softies!

You will need
- Sewing kit (see pages 112–113)
- US6 (4mm) knitting needles
- Balls of DK yarn:
- Tapestry needle
- Poly fill

How to knit a hero

Knit stripes

Use stockinette stitch (see page 121). Begin with the legs.
STRIPE 1: Cast on 28 stitches in leg color. Work 11 rows, starting with knit stitch.
STRIPE 2: Change to shorts color. Work 7 rows.
STRIPE 3: Change to belt color. Work 1 row.
STRIPE 4: Change to vest color. Work 10 rows.
STRIPE 5: Change to face color. Work 7 rows.
STRIPE 6: Change to mask color. Work 4 rows.
STRIPE 7: Change to hat color. Work 7 rows.
Cast off.

Knitted stripes

7
6
5
4
3
2
1

Cast on 28 stitches.

1 Fold the knitting in half and sew the edges, right-sides together.

2 Bring the seam to the center and sew the top end together.

NOTE: TO MAKE ROUND-SHAPED HEADS
Stitch around the top edge of the knitting, pull on the thread to gather it, secure the thread, and cut off.

3 Turn right-side out, fill the shape, and sew the bottom closed.

4 Pull the end of the yarn tight, then sew extra stitches to keep it in place.

Sew a running stitch around the base of the face stripe. Gather to make a rounded head shape.

Secure the yarn tightly.

Shape arms and legs

To make the arm and leg shapes, sew through the body as indicated by the dotted lines.

Hold the doll's body where the legs will be.

Bring the needle from front to back.

Sew down to the feet area and fasten off.

Adding features

Once the doll is complete, add personal touches. See the steps on page 69 to learn how to sew the eyes, mouth, and nose.

Repeat for the arms. Position as indicated by the dotted lines.

Shape the hat

Shape the peaks and pin them in position.

Make a face

Use yarn to make the eyes and mouth.

Pinch the corner of the head and sew across to form a peak.

Action Boy

Make a symbol with three stitches.

Zombie Alien

To make her braids, thread three strands of yarn at the side of the head and braid.

► KNIT 7 STRIPES
1: 4 rows
2: 1 row
3: 10 rows
4: 1 row
5: 1 row
6: 21 rows
7: 4 rows

Mystery Hero

Use single stitches for each eye and the mouth.

Use two stitches for each eye.

◄ KNIT 6 STRIPES
1: 4 rows
2: 12 rows
3: 2 rows
4: 11 rows
5: 6 rows
6: 11 rows

► KNIT 5 STRIPES
1: 4 rows
2: 12 rows
3: 13 rows
4: 10 rows
5: 10 rows

Colorful characters

These are created by changing the color and depth of the stripes (see page 83). Starting with the feet, cast on 28 stitches and follow the number of stripes and rows for each one.

Action Girl

Jolly Roger

Make a patch with black yarn.

► KNIT 11 STRIPES
1: 4 rows
2: 10 rows
3: 2 rows
4: 2 rows
5: 2 rows
6: 2 rows
7: 2 rows
8: 2 rows
9: 1 row
10: 13 rows
11: 5 rows

Ninja Kid

► KNIT 6 STRIPES
1: 15 rows
2: 2 rows
3: 18 rows
4: 3 rows
5: 2 rows
6: 7 rows

Add Ninja features by attaching yarn to the head and to the waist.

Cool Dude

► KNIT 9 STRIPES
1: 4 rows
2: 12 rows
3: 7 rows
4: 2 rows
5: 11 rows
6: 8 rows
7: 2 rows
8: 2 rows
9: 3 rows

You will need
- Piece of cardboard 8in x 3in (20cm x 8cm)
- Balls of colorful yarn
- Scissors

Multi-colored dolls

This project is a great way to use up scraps of yarn. Start by wrapping the yarn around the cardboard, as shown. Add a new color when the first one runs out.

Yarn dolls

Make dolls that dance delightfully! With this simple project, transform colorful leftover yarns into fun swaying dolls.

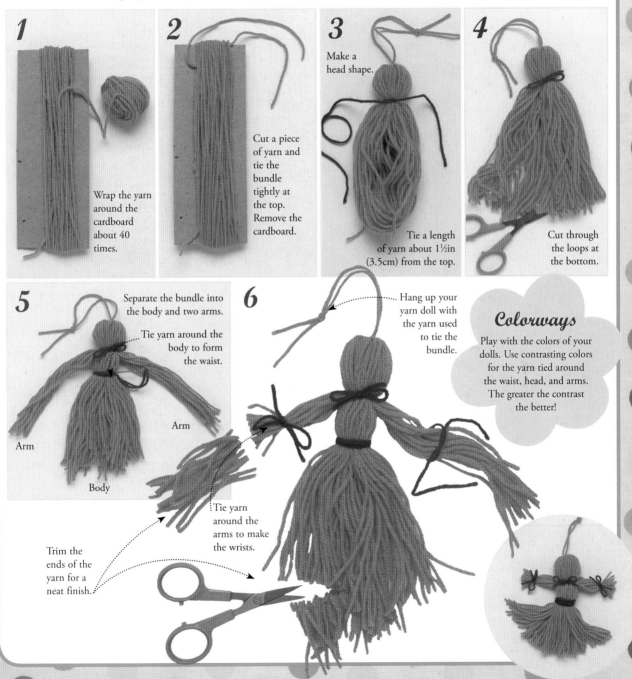

1 Wrap the yarn around the cardboard about 40 times.

2 Cut a piece of yarn and tie the bundle tightly at the top. Remove the cardboard.

3 Make a head shape.

Tie a length of yarn about 1½in (3.5cm) from the top.

4 Cut through the loops at the bottom.

5 Separate the bundle into the body and two arms.

Tie yarn around the body to form the waist.

Arm

Arm

Body

6 Hang up your yarn doll with the yarn used to tie the bundle.

Trim the ends of the yarn for a neat finish.

Tie yarn around the arms to make the wrists.

Colorways

Play with the colors of your dolls. Use contrasting colors for the yarn tied around the waist, head, and arms. The greater the contrast the better!

3

Dolly
mixtures

Lavender girls

Here's a fresh take on lavender sachets. Hang these dolls filled with aromatic herbs in your closet and give your clothes a sweet scent.

You will need

- Sewing kit (see pages 112–113) BODY PARTS •
Scraps of felt fabric DRESS • Cotton fabric 5in x 5in
(13cm x 13cm) • 2 tbsp dried lavender • Paper for
funnel • Ribbon 9in (23cm) • Button • Pinking shears

1

Prepare the doll pieces.

Using tracing paper, trace over the shapes on the following page.

Cut out the paper pieces, pin to the fabric, and cut out the fabric.

Use pinking shears to keep the edges from fraying.

2

Embroidery thread

Leave the top open.

Dried lavender

Sew the two dress pieces together using running stitch, leaving an opening at the top.

Make a funnel out of paper and place it in the opening. Pour the lavender into the dress.

3

Place the top of the dress between the head pieces and pin in place.

Sew all the layers together.

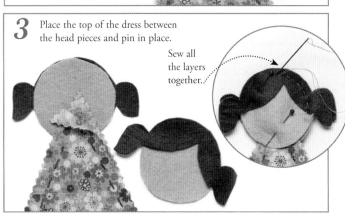

Sew two arm pieces together.

Attach the arms to the back of the dress.

Bring the hands to the front.

Fold both leg pieces in half and sew together.

Attach the legs to the back of the dress.

Place the edge of each leg in the center of a shoe shape.

Fold the shoe over and sew the two sides together.

HAIR BACK
Cut 1

HAIR FRONT
Cut 1

HEAD Cut 2

LEGS Cut 2

DRESS Cut 2

Remember to place the
paper pattern along
the fold of the fabric.

ARMS Cut 4

FOLD LINE for fabric

SHOES Cut 2

Ribbon

Place the ends of
the ribbon at the back
of the head and sew
them in place with the
button on the front.

Template

The shapes on this page are
all you need to make your
lavender doll. Place a piece
of tracing paper over the
page and trace around the
shapes. Cut them out and lay the
shapes on the fabric.

More lavender ladies

Rickrack ribbon

Different dollies
Make these dolls in the same way as the doll shown on pages 90–91. Follow the steps and add the variations you like.

VEIL
Cut a strip of netting, gather it along the edge, and sew it all the way around the head.

FANCY RIBBON
Sew the ribbon to the bottom of the dress and around the neck. Use it to finish the headdress.

White cotton dress

Lavender Bride

BOUQUET
To make a bouquet, cut small disks of felt using pinking shears. Sew a felt flower shape onto the disks. Sew the bouquet onto the dress.

FUNKY LEGS
Coordinate the legs, shoes, and hair by making them in accent colors from the dress.

Lavender Girl

Place your doll on a coat hanger and hang her in your closet.

Lavender Fairy

A band of felt makes the crown.

Use pinking shears to create fancy edges.

Fairy wings

Fold a piece of felt 2½in x 3¼in (6cm x 8cm) in half. Use pinking shears to cut an oval shape. Open out the shape, place it in the center of the fairy's back, and neatly sew it to the dress down the middle of the wings.

Pull the thread to gather the fabric. This will give the legs shape.

Doodle dolls

Bring your doodles to life by tracing the drawings onto fabric to create fun-shaped pillows.

1 Using the permanent marker, draw doodles on a piece of paper.

2 Cut a piece of fabric larger than each one of your doodles. Leave a 2in (5cm) space around the edges of your drawing.

Place the fabric over your doodle.

Using a permanent marker, trace over the drawing. You can also draw a doodle right onto the fabric.

You will need
- Sewing kit (see pages 112–113)
- Paper and pens for doodling
- White cotton fabric
- Colorful cotton fabric
- Permanent markers for drawing on fabric • Pencil
- Poly fill

3 Turn the fabric over so the drawing is showing reverse-side up. ......

Draw a pencil line ¾in (2cm) away from the image. .....

4 Take a piece of colorful fabric, right-side up, and lay the drawing on top.

Pin the pieces of fabric together.

: Use running stitch to sew along the pencil outline.

.......Leave an opening at the bottom.

Picture size

If your doodles aren't the size you want, reduce or enlarge them on a photocopier. Trace over the revised image size.

TIP:
Leaving the extra space around your drawing allows it to sit on top of the pillow and not disappear over the sides.

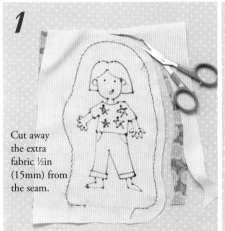

1

Cut away the extra fabric ½in (15mm) from the seam.

2

Turn the drawing right-side out.

Fill up the doll so it's nicely padded.

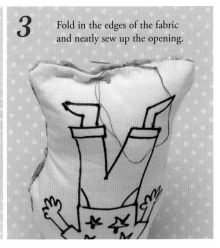

3

Fold in the edges of the fabric and neatly sew up the opening.

Small doodle dolls make good pin cushions and needle holders.

Bright fabric backing

To add color to your dolls, mix and match the backing fabric. Any lightweight cotton will work well.

Colorful Characters

Complete your doodle dolls by coloring them in. Use permanent markers or fabric pens and color in the drawings, just as you would on paper.

I'm a princess. I'm even more beautiful in color!

Little Lotties

Every Lottie needs a Little Lottie and maybe even a Baby Lottie, too. Sew a drawstring bag where you can keep them all.

You will need
- Sewing kit (see page 112–113)
- Felt in assorted colors
- Poly fill
- Cotton fabric for dresses and bags

How to make Little Lotties

Little Lottie templates

Lay tracing paper over the shapes. Trace over the lines and cut out the shapes.

Baby Lottie templates

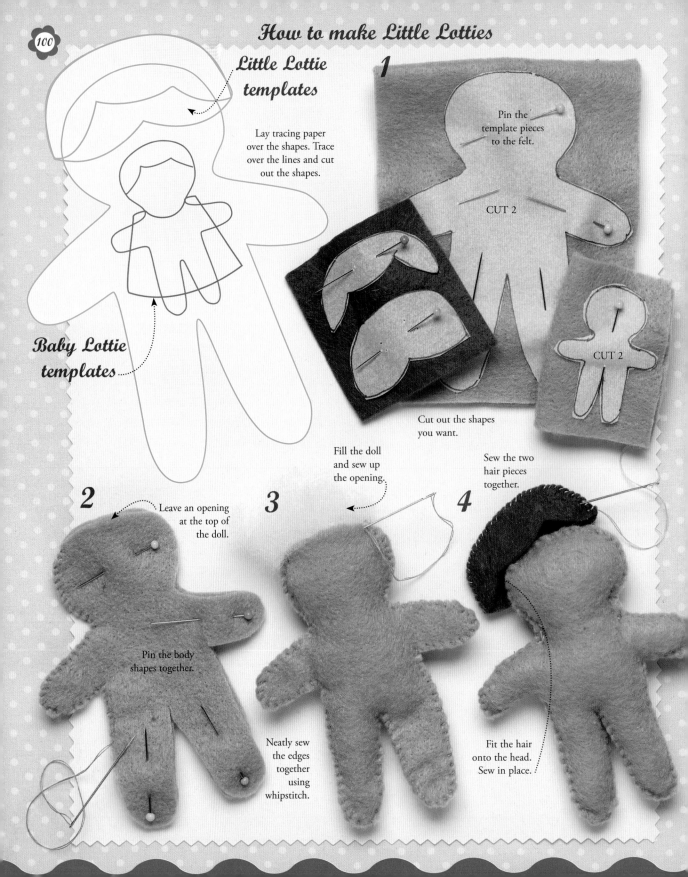

1 Pin the template pieces to the felt.

CUT 2

CUT 2

Cut out the shapes you want.

2 Leave an opening at the top of the doll.

Pin the body shapes together.

Neatly sew the edges together using whipstitch.

3 Fill the doll and sew up the opening.

4 Sew the two hair pieces together.

Fit the hair onto the head. Sew in place.

How to make Baby Lotties

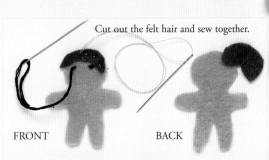

Cut out two doll shapes.

Cut out the felt hair and sew together.

FRONT   BACK

Sew the hair and face to the front piece.

Place the front and back pieces together.

Sew them together using small running stitches.

Cut out two dress shapes and two bows.

BOWS

DRESS

Dolly bags

Each doll can have its very own drawstring bag. Find out how to make the bags on page 102.

On the doll, sew the dress pieces together at the shoulders and under the arms.

Add little felt shapes to the dress for decoration.

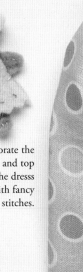

Decorate the edge and top of the dresss with fancy stitches.

Finishing your Little Lottie

Make a face and add bows

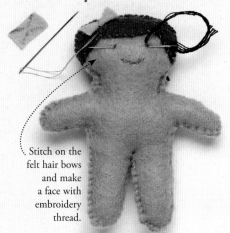

Stitch on the felt hair bows and make a face with embroidery thread.

See page 19 for more about making faces.

Make a dress

1 Cut a piece of fabric 6in x 2¾in (15cm x 6.5cm). Place right-side down.

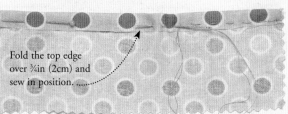

Fold the top edge over ¾in (2cm) and sew in position.

2 Bring the sides to the middle of the fabric.

Cut slits on the edge on each side to make arm holes.

3 Cut a ribbon 11in (28cm) long.

Pass the safety pin and ribbon through the hem at the top.

Attach a safety pin to the end of the ribbon.

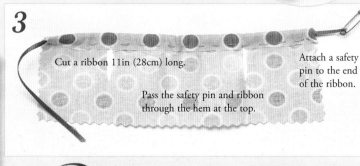

Make a bag

See page 32 for more about making bags.

Make a carrier bag for your dolls. Cut a piece of fabric 9in x 6½in (23cm x 16cm). Fold it in half and sew along the bottom and side. Fold over the top edge ¾in (2cm). Sew the folded edge down and pass a length of ribbon through the gap.

Mix and match dolls

Match the baby to the doll. The variations for these little dolls are endless, so experiment with colors and fabrics.

Cut out tiny bows and felt shapes to decorate the dolls.

Finish the edges with pinking shears.

Pillow dolls

Plump up the pillows! Draw square and rectangular shapes and create characters inside the lines.

1 Cut out a piece of white cotton fabric 7in (18cm) x 7in (18cm).

First, draw a pillow-doll picture on paper.

Copy or trace your image onto the fabric.

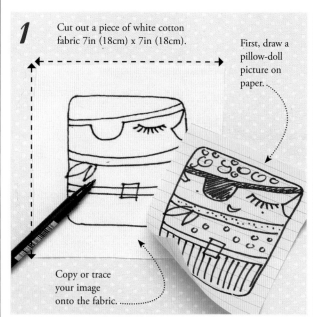

2 Cut a piece of patterned fabric the same size as the white cotton square.

Pin the two pieces together, right sides facing.

Using backstitch, sew all the way around, ½in (15mm) away from the fabric edge. Leave a gap at the bottom.

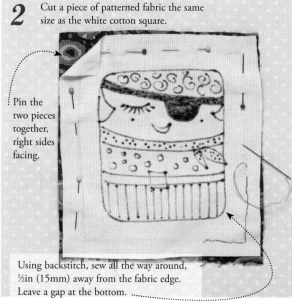

3 Turn the pillow right-side out.

Fill the pillow, fold the edges in, then sew them together neatly.

4

Color in the pillow and add buttons, if you like, for decoration.

This view shows the pillow dolls' plump shape and pretty fabric backing.

Handy dolls

Create helpful hideaways!

These dolls will make handy covers for your scissors. They also look pretty as key rings.

7 Undo the pin and knot the ribbon ends.

6 Push the safety pin through the gap in the seam from the inside.

Trace the outline of this template onto tracing paper.

1 Cut out the template and pin it to the felt.

Cut out two body shapes.

Cut out any other felt shapes you're using.

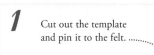
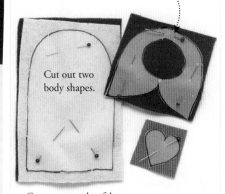

2 Complete the front first.

Sew all your felt shapes to the front piece only; use running stitch.

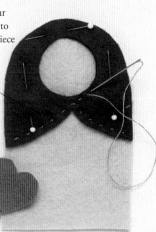

3 Pin on the back and sew around the shape.

Leave a small gap in the stitches to allow room for the ribbon.

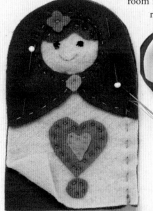

Whipstitch the ends so the felt pieces don't come apart.

5 Attach a safety pin through the two ends of the ribbon.

4 Fold the ribbon in half. Bring the folded end through the scissors. Pass the ends of the ribbon though the loop and pull tight.

You will need
- Tracing paper and pen for the template
- Sewing kit (see pages 112–113)
- Colorful felt fabric
- Ribbon 28in (70cm)

Hideaway
To make your scissors disappear, pull the ribbon up. To make them reappear, grab them and pull down.

Alien

Flower Girl

Jolly Pirate

For the body template, see page 106.

Handy features

Trace around these shapes to create the characters above. For the main part of the body, use the template on the previous page.

Jolly Pirate's hat

Jolly Pirate's eyepatch and scarf

Robot

Super Boy

What's hiding?

Check that the template is big enough to hide away your object. If you need to make it larger, enlarge it on a photocopier.

Bedtime Dolly

Super Boy's mask

Super Boy's belt

Alien's eyes

Bedtime Dolly's flowers and bow

Robot's eyes and mouth

4

Knitting and sewing know-how

Creating dolls

For each project in this book, you'll find a list of everything you need to make it. The most essential piece of equipment is the sewing kit—have this ready at all times. Also shown here are some other items you'll find useful.

You will need

Each project will begin by listing the materials required to make it.

Know-how

The pages at the back of the book will help explain different sewing and knitting techniques.

Sewing kit

Here are the sewing essentials— keep them together in a handy box.

Sewing needles

Needle threader

Safety pin

Tapestry needles

Needles

Use tapestry needles with large eyes and rounded ends for knitting yarn. Sewing needles with large eyes and pointed ends work best with sewing and embroidery thread.

Sewing thread

Keep an array of colorful threads on hand as well as the basic colors like black, gray, and brown.

Pins

These are glass-headed dressmaking pins.

Scissors

Use small sharp embroidery scissors to snip off threads and cut out tiny doll shapes.

Tape measure

You will need this to measure your fabric at the start of a project, and to help you position pieces accurately.

Thimble

On big projects, doing a lot of hand-stitching can make your middle finger sore—use the thimble on this finger to push the needle through fabric.

Ribbons

Ribbons work well for decoration. They are also useful for gathering fabric to make skirts and bags, and for fastening clothes.

Felt fabric

Felt is very versatile. It's easy to shape and doesn't fray when you cut it—perfect for tiny projects like these shoes.

Poly fill

This polyester fiber is used for all the projects in this book. It's very soft and can be worked easily into all the different doll shapes.

Embroidery thread

This thread is thick, so use it when you want to make stitches that show, or for stitches that are purely decorative.

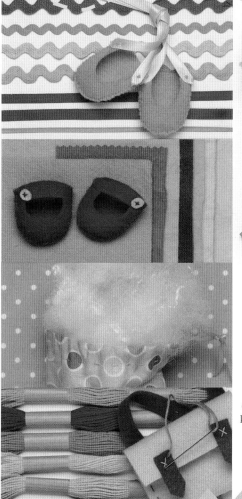

DK (double-knit) yarn

Knitting needles US6 (4mm)

Knitting yarn and needles

All the knitting projects use DK (double-knit) yarn and size US6 (4mm) knitting needles. How much yarn? Most projects are small, so it might be possible to use up your leftovers. To make it simple, each project refers to balls of yarn for each color.

Stitch holder.

Large scissors

For cutting out templates and larger pieces of fabric, these scissors are ideal. Sharp scissors are easier to use than blunt ones and produce the best results.

Pinking shears

These scissors prevent cotton fabric from fraying because their blades are zigzag shaped. The effect is attractive as well and can be used for decoration.

How to stitch

Here are the stitches used in the projects. They all have a different job to do when you are sewing fabric together for pillows, bags, and patchwork pieces.

How to start and finish

Begin sewing with a knot at the end of the thread. To end a row of stitches, make a tiny stitch, but do not pull it tight. Bring the thread back up through the loop and pull tight. Do this once more in the same spot, then cut the thread.

Running stitch

This is a very versatile stitch used for seams, sewing fabric together, and gathering.

Keep the stitches and the spaces between them small and even.

Backstitch

This is the strongest stitch. It makes a continuous line of stitches so it is best for joining two pieces of fabric securely, such as the sides of a bag.

Make the stitch, then bring the needle back to the place where the last stitch is finished.

VIEW FROM REVERSE

Bring the needle out, ready to begin the next stitch.

Basting stitch

This is a temporary stitch. It will be removed but it is useful for holding pieces of fabric in place before you sew them together permanently. It is also called a tacking stitch.

Basting stitches are like running stitches, but larger and they don't need to be even.

Whipstitch

These are tiny, neat, and even stitches that are almost invisible. Use them to top-sew two finished edges together, such as when you are joining patchwork pieces.

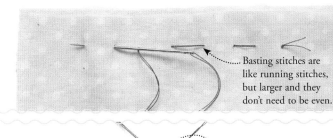

Insert the needle diagonally from the back of the fabric.

Pick up only two or three threads of fabric.

Slip stitch

Use slip stitch when you want the stitches to be invisible. This stitch is made by slipping the thread under a fold of fabric. It is often used to join two folded edges, such as the openings of pillows.

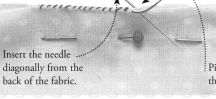

Slide the needle into the fold of the fabric.

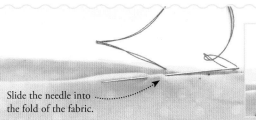

Bring the needle out, then slide the needle in the other side.

Lazy daisy stitch

This pretty stitch is very useful for embroidery decoration. Draw your daisy design in light pencil first, then follow the lines with your stitches.

1 Tie a knot in your thread and pull it up through the beginning of a petal and down at the end.

2 Next, bring it up through another petal until you have finished the flower.

Chain stitch

This is a very useful decorating stitch—great for flower stems and leaves. You may need to practice the stitch to get it just right.

1 Tie a knot in the thread and pull it up through the fabric.

2 Push the needle back down next to the thread.

3 Don't pull it tight; leave a little loop.

5 Repeat Steps 1 to 4, keeping the stitches as even as possible.

4 Bring the needle up through the loop and pull the thread through.

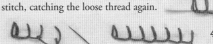

Practice chain stitch on a curved line so you can make shapes.

Blanket stitch

This stitch is good for making neat, decorative edges and for sewing one piece of fabric to another.

1 Tie a knot in the thread and pull the needle up through the fabric.

2 Push the needle back through next to the stitch and up below it, making sure the loose end is caught, as shown.

3 Push the needle down and up again so it is the same size as the previous stitch, catching the loose thread again.

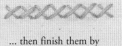

4 Repeat these steps to make more loops.

Cross-stitch

You can make entire pictures using cross-stitch.

1 Draw crosses in light pencil on your fabric.

2 Sew a line of crosses from left to right in one direction...

... then finish them by sewing back the other way.

Sewing tip

For best results, keep your stitches neat and even.

Finishing

On the back of the fabric, push the needle through the loop of the last stitch.

Pull the thread tight and repeat to secure it.

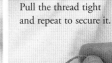

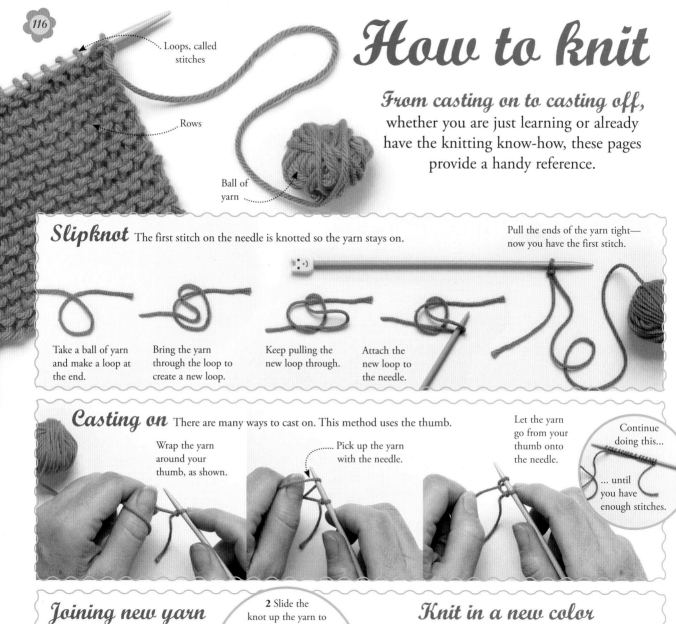

Loops, called stitches

Rows

Ball of yarn

How to knit

From casting on to casting off, whether you are just learning or already have the knitting know-how, these pages provide a handy reference.

Slipknot
The first stitch on the needle is knotted so the yarn stays on.

Pull the ends of the yarn tight—now you have the first stitch.

Take a ball of yarn and make a loop at the end.

Bring the yarn through the loop to create a new loop.

Keep pulling the new loop through.

Attach the new loop to the needle.

Casting on
There are many ways to cast on. This method uses the thumb.

Wrap the yarn around your thumb, as shown.

Pick up the yarn with the needle.

Let the yarn go from your thumb onto the needle.

Continue doing this...

... until you have enough stitches.

Joining new yarn

Do this when adding a new ball of yarn or making stripes.

2 Slide the knot up the yarn to the needle.

1 Tie the new yarn to the old yarn with a loose knot.

3 Continue knitting as usual.

Knit in a new color

Here, the knitting is shown on the reverse side. Join the new yarn, as shown (left). To neaten the loose ends of both colors, gather them with the working yarn as you knit.

Stitches 1, 2, 3, 4, 5 ...

How many?

The projects in this book tell you how many stitches to cast on. Many stitches produce a wide fabric, while a few stitches create a narrow fabric.

When you are starting a new row, begin with the first stitch on the right and work toward the left.

The yarn will also be on the right.

Getting started

You will need to cast on the number of stitches required in the pattern. The stitches that are being worked will be on the left-hand needle, and the ones you have made will go on the right.

Casting off

Begin the row by knitting two stitches.

Pick up the first stitch with the left needle.

Carry this first stitch over the second stitch and over the end of the needle.

Repeat Steps 1–3...

... until one stitch remains. Open up the loop.

Cut the yarn and place the end in the loop.

Pull the yarn to close the loop.

Neaten ends

Sew in the loose ends when adding new yarn or neatening the loose ends of finished pieces.

Use this method when neatening seams or knitting stripes.

Thread the end with a tapestry needle.

Sew the thread into the edge of the knitting.

Bring the needle out and cut the yarn.

Use this method when neatening loose ends of finished pieces.

Thread the needle onto the loose end and sew down the side of the knitting.

Bring the needle out and cut the yarn.

Knit stitch

Another name for knit stitch is plain stitch. Simple to make and regularly used in many projects, it is the most common stitch.

Method 1

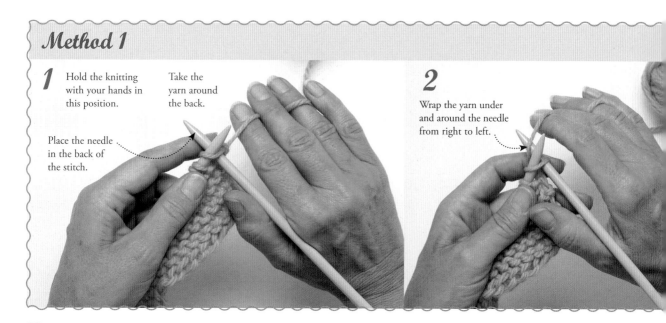

1 Hold the knitting with your hands in this position.

Take the yarn around the back.

Place the needle in the back of the stitch.

2 Wrap the yarn under and around the needle from right to left.

Method 2
This method might be easier for left-handed knitters.

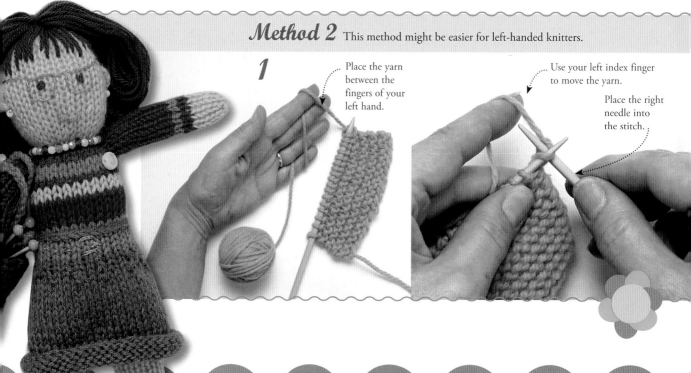

1 Place the yarn between the fingers of your left hand.

Use your left index finger to move the yarn.

Place the right needle into the stitch.

Garter Stitch

Garter stitch isn't an actual stitch but the name given to a piece of knitting where every row is knitted in knit stitch. The effect is bobbly on both sides.

You can also make garter stitch if you knit every row in purl stitch.

3 Pull on the yarn and move the needle from the back to the front.

4 The right needle is now on top of the left one and has taken the stitch with it.

5 Slide the top needle to the right. The stitch will now be transferred onto the right needle, completing the stitch.

Begin the next stitch as in step 1.

3 Bring the yarn down firmly between the needles.

4 Bring the needle with the loop of yarn to the front.

5 Take the needle with the stitch off the left-hand needle.

Begin the next stitch as in step 1.

For purl stitch, the needle goes in the front of the stitch.

The yarn goes at the front, too.

Purl stitch

Work from the front. This stitch is made by the needle going in the front of the stitch. When knit and purl stitch rows are alternated the knitting looks smooth.

Method 1

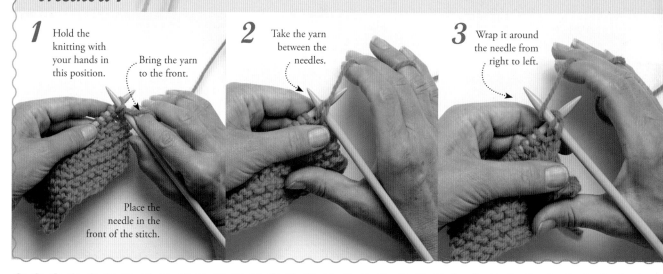

1 Hold the knitting with your hands in this position.

Bring the yarn to the front.

Place the needle in the front of the stitch.

2 Take the yarn between the needles.

3 Wrap it around the needle from right to left.

Method 2 This method is often easier for left-handers.

1 Hold the knitting in your left hand, with the yarn at the front of the work.

Place the right-hand needle in the front of the stitch.

2 Wind the yarn around the front of the needle.

3 Wind the yarn around again.

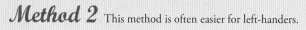

Purl stitch + Knit stitch = Stockinette stitch

Stockinette stitch isn't an actual stitch at all. Instead, it is made by working a knit row then a purl row, a knit row then a purl row, and so on. The result is a smooth front to the knitting and a knobby back.

BACK
The purl-stitch side

FRONT
The knit-stitch side

4 Pull on the yarn and move the needle from front to back...

5 ... taking the stitch with it.

6 Take the rest of the yarn off the needle to complete the stitch.

Begin the next stitch as in Step 1.

4 Bring the right-hand needle from front to back, taking the yarn with it.

5 Pull the rest of the stitch off the needle.

6 Now you are ready to begin the next stitch, starting at Step 1 again.

Threading needles

NEEDLE TYPES

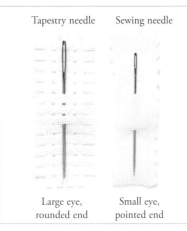

Tapestry needle   Sewing needle

Large eye,   Small eye,
rounded end   pointed end

THREADING EMBROIDERY THREAD OR WOOL YARN

1 Loop the thread over a tapestry needle, pull tight, and remove the needle.

Keep the looped yarn pinched tightly between your finger and thumb.

2 Bring the eye of the needle over the top of the yarn.

3 Pull the loop of yarn though the eye of the needle.

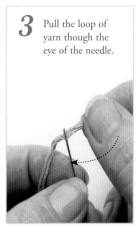

USING A NEEDLE THREADER

1 Push the threader wire through the eye of the sewing needle.

Put the end of the thread though the wire.

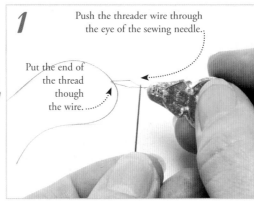

2 Pull the wire and thread through the eye.

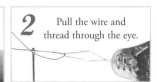

3 Remove the wire.

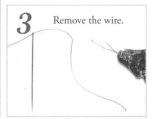

Handy tip

If you work with thread that is too long it will get tangled, slowing you down. Work with thread that is roughly the length from your fingertips to your elbow.

Sewing on a button

1

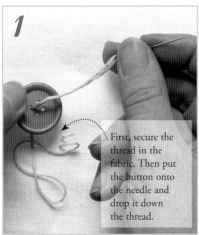

First, secure the thread in the fabric. Then put the button onto the needle and drop it down the thread.

2 Push the needle back through the holes in the button.

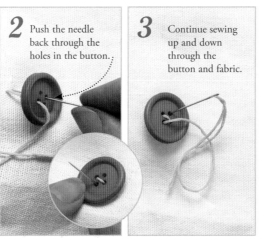

3 Continue sewing up and down through the button and fabric.

4

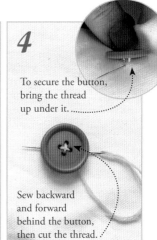

To secure the button, bring the thread up under it.

Sew backward and forward behind the button, then cut the thread.

Crochet chain stitch

Use this method to make the handles for the bags on page 70.

Refer to page 116 to find out how to make a loop.

HOW TO HOLD

Wrap the yarn around your left hand as shown here.

Hold the hook in your right hand.

Transfer the loop onto the hook and pull gently on the yarn.

1 Hold the slipknot firmly between finger and thumb. ....

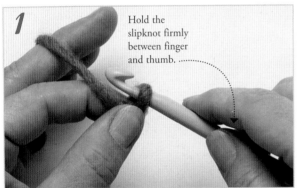

2 Push the hook under the yarn and catch it with the hook. ....

3 Pull the hook back through the stitch. .

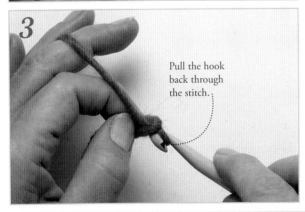

4 The stitch is complete. .

5 Repeat Steps 1–4 to continue the chain.

Make as many chain stitches as the pattern requires.

This foundation chain has 10 stitches—count the "V" shapes.

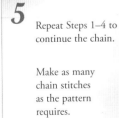

1   2   3   4   5   6   7   8   9   10